PAPERBACK PARNASSUS

PAPERBACK PARNASSUS

- The Birth -
- The Development -
- The Pending Crisis . . . of the Modern American
Paperbound Book -

Roger H. Smith

WESTVIEW PRESS

Published in 1976 in the United States of America by

Westview Press, Inc.
1898 Flatiron Court
Boulder, Colorado 80301
Frederick A. Praeger, Publisher and Editorial Director

Library of Congress Cataloging in Publication Data

Smith, Roger H
   Paperback Parnassus.

   Bibliography: p.
   Includes index.
   1. Bibliography--Paperback editions. 2. Book
industries and trade--United States--History. I. Title.
Z1033.P3S6   016.0705'73   75-37585
ISBN 0-89158-007-7

Printed and bound in the United States of America.
Jacket design adapted from a cartoon by ERDOES, courtesy of the
artist's agent, John Locke, 15 East 76th Street, New York, NY 10021.

For *Mildred C. Smith*

Acknowledgements

This book grew out of a series of articles about paperback distribution which I wrote and which *Publishers Weekly* published in March and April of 1975. The idea for the series came from Lila Freilicher, assistant editor of *PW,* and to her I wish to express special thanks. Other *PW* colleagues offered help, criticism and encouragement when my enthusiasm was flagging; among them Arnold W. Ehrlich, Chandler B. Grannis, Jean Norrington and Miriam Phelps.

Many people in the paperback industry, in granting me interviews and behind-the-scenes scenarios, were generous with their time and their counsel. I want to thank particularly Stanley Budner, Ronald Busch, Edward L. Butler, Joe Byrne, Ross Claiborne, Alun Davies, Robert Fair de Graff, John Dessauer, Robert G. Diforio, Oscar Dystel, Sidney Graedon, Dr. Donald Hauss, Howard Kaminski, Abe Koppleman, Freeman Lewis, Esther Margolis, Peter M. Mayer, Helen Meyer, John Meszaros, David Moscow, Patrick O'Connor, Ed Pendergast, Russell Reynolds, Gerald Rubinsky, Louis Satz, Herbert K. Schnall, Leon Shimkin, Roysce Smith, Richard Snyder, Carl W. Tobey, George Wright and Francis Zinni. Whatever collective wisdom is in this book is theirs. The mistakes, of course, are mine.

In writing this book, I discovered, as many writers have already discovered, that my family's greatest contribution was to stay away quietly while I engaged in prolonged bouts of brooding and/or composition. For this, my thanks to Beverly and to Roger and William.

Roger H. Smith
Amagansett, N.Y.
September 7, 1975

Glossary

AAP	Association of American Publishers
ABA	American Booksellers Association
CID	Council for Independent Distribution
CPDA	Council for Periodical Distributors Associations
FTC	Federal Trade Commission
ID	Independent Wholesaler
NACS	National Association of College Stores
PBIP	*Paperbound Books in Print*
PW	*Publishers Weekly*
UPC	Universal Product Code

Contents

1   *Paperback Parnassus* 1

2   *Two Paperback Worlds: Mass Market and Trade* 7

3   *How the Books Arrive* 11

4   *Distribution Comes of Age, or Atrophy* 15

5   *The Anatomy of Waste* 25

6   *IDs: A Composite Portrait* 33

7   *What Future for Export?* 39

8   *Birth, Life and Death in the Mass Market* 49

9   *Quick History of an "Extra"* 61

10   *Boom and Bust and Boom and . . .* 65

11   *Trade Paperbacks: To Academe and Beyond* 77

12   *The News of the Month in Review* 83

13   *Neurosis and the Crisis of 1974-75* 87

14   *The Cloudy Crystal Ball* 91

Appendix 102

Chapter 1
Paperback Parnassus

Paperback Parnassus is an extraordinary bookstore located in an extraordinary shopping center. In addition to the usual stores selling food, shoes, medicines, clothing for men, women and children, haircuts and permanent waves, the shopping center includes several churches which are very active every day, an elementary and a secondary school and a community college, a bowling alley and a pool hall, a chess club and a bridge club, a gym, a movie theater, a few restaurants and a saloon. The shopping center is open 24 hours a day, seven days a week; so is the bookstore.

Paperback Parnassus is housed in a building with about the same square footage as an airplane hangar. As the name suggests, it sells paperback books—only paperback books. On several miles of shelves, it displays over 123,000 titles, from *A: A Novel* by Andy Warhol to *Zwingli: A Reformed Theologian* by Jacques Courvoisier. Warhol, we assume, cared about leading the parade, and Zwingli's splendidly named biographer was pleased to be the banquet's last course.

Paperback Parnassus

The books are displayed in 26 major subject classifications*
and several hundred subclassifications, according to a scheme
that the American Booksellers Association and the National
Association of College Stores worked out in 1962 to assist their
members in stocking their paperback departments. At one
time, arrangement would have been by publishers' lines. That
was convenient for publishers' salesmen and store personnel in
checking inventory. But it was inconvenient for customers,
who rarely knew who had published a book they wanted, and
became impractical as the number of lines grew. Over 2700
publishers' imprints are represented at Paperback Parnassus.

Despite the large subject-heading signs above the racks, a
browser coming into Paperback Parnassus for the first time
will be bewildered and then overwhelmed by the magnitude of
the whole thing. He may wonder why there are 19 different
editions of Shakespeare's *Hamlet,* 15 of *The Aeneid,* 15 of
Gulliver's Travels, 14 of *Great Expectations,* 14 of *Candide,* 12
of *Crime and Punishment,* 12 of *Madame Bovary,* 11 of *The
Divine Comedy,* nine of *Silas Marner.* Is this some kind of
overkill? Perhaps not, since each book has its own
introduction, its own critical approach, its own pedagogical
apparatus.

The largest group of titles consists of manuals for passing
every conceivable kind of Civil Service test. The second largest
contains books by and about Shakespeare. There are great
arrays of art books, atlases, Bibles and Bible study books,
books about blacks, cookbooks, dictionaries, encyclopedias
on all kinds of subjects.

A woman shopper, looking ahead to a summer by the sea,
can pick up several score of crossword puzzle books to sustain
her. Since she plans to spend as little time in the kitchen as

*Art, Biography, Business, Cooking, Crafts, Drama, Education, Fiction,
Games, History, Humor, Juvenile, Language, Literature, Medicine, Music,
Nature, Philosophy, Poetry, Political Science, Psychology, Reference,
Religion, Science, Sociology, Travel.

possible, she might find the simplicity of *Quick Frozen Peas* appealing. For cloudy days at the shore, she might like to have *Random Walks* on hand, but beware, for this is a textbook full of charts and statistics and therefore unlikely to help in country rambles.

For her children, she can pick up 25 *Dennis the Menace* cartoon books, 19 of *Pogo* and 17 of *B.C.* If she is really serious about the kids, she would do well to get down to basics and get a copy of *Growing Up With Paperbacks.*

Her husband, when he comes to spend his vacation with his family, might like to read *Falstaff's Complete Beer Book* or, if that is not strong enough, *Hashish: Its Chemistry and Pharmacology.* He needs a new hobby, she thinks, and *Preparation and Use of Weather Maps by Mariners* might get him started. Certainly better than *Unusual Sex Practices* or *Nymphomania: A Study of the Oversexed Woman.*

The authors who have the most titles in paperback make an interesting, if somewhat inconclusive, study. Among the classics, there is Shakespeare, of course, and also Aesop, Aristotle, William Blake, the Brontës, Chaucer, Dickens, Dostoevsky, Fielding, Homer, Milton, Rousseau, Sophocles. For the Germans, Thomas Mann. For the French, Balzac, Flaubert, Gide, Victor Hugo, Mauriac, Maurois, Molière, Sartre, Stendhal. Paperback prolifics from England include Lewis Carroll, Galsworthy, Graham Greene, D.H. Lawrence, George Orwell, H.G. Wells.

The whole history of American literature is here: Hawthorne, Melville, Thoreau, Poe, Cooper, Henry James, Dreiser, Jack London; Faulkner, Hemingway, Fitzgerald, Dos Passos, O'Hara; Henry Miller, Norman Mailer, Kurt Vonnegut, Jr., John Updike.

Over at the Western counter, saddled up and ready to write are Max Brand, Ernest Haycox, Louis L'Amour, William M. Raine, Zane Grey.

Bridge with Charles Goren? Chess with Fred Reinfeld? Spiritual uplift with Billy Graham? Worlds of the future with Isaac Asimov, James Brill (*Star Trek*), Robert Heinlein, Robert Silverberg? Romance, terror and a nice little cry with Charlotte Armstrong, Dorothy Eden, Barbara Cartland, Georgette Heyer, June Hodge, Victoria Holt, Norah Lofts, Mary Stewart?

Skulking around the mystery and adventure department at Paperback Parnassus is a large group of prolific writers, perhaps the largest group in the store, assembled under the avuncular eye of Arthur Conan Doyle, with Agatha Christie as den mother. Here are Edward S. Aarons, Philip Atlee, Carter Brown, Leslie Charteris, John Creasey, Ian Fleming, Erle Stanley Gardner, Brett Halliday, Donald Hamilton, John D. MacDonald, Ross Macdonald, Dan J. Marlowe, J.J. Marric, Ngaio Marsh, Don Pendleton, Richard S. Prather, Ellery Queen, Mary Roberts Rinehart, Mickey Spillane, Rex Stout.

All is not belles lettres. Some prolific paperback "authors" have names like the Acme School of Aeronautics, Airframe and Powerplant, the American Library Association, (Chilton) Automotive Editorial Department, Boy Scouts of America, Committee for Economic Development, Congressional Quarterly Service, Daughters of St. Paul, Girl Scouts of the U.S.A., Eastman Kodak, *Playboy* and *Sunset*.

A cross-disciplinary "most prolific" list produces some strange juxtapositions: Faith Baldwin and James Baldwin, Donald R. Brann (home repairs) and Keith L. Brooks (Bible study), Erskine Caldwell and Taylor Caldwell, Dale Carnegie and Fidel Castro, Sri Chinmoy (guru stuff) and Kahlil Gibran, Margaret Farrar (crosswords) and William M. Gaines (*Mad* magazine), Arlene Hale (nurses) and Alfred Hitchcock, Ted Mark ("Man from O.R.G.Y." series) and Karl Marx, Margaret Mead and Lewis Mumford, Ed Radlauer (bicycle, motorcycle and car racing) and G.T. Ridion (family trees).

4

Paperback Parnassus does not exist as an actual store, of course. Rather, we have been strolling through *Paperbound Books in Print*, the most complete bibliography listing available U.S. titles and those from abroad which have regular U.S. distributors. *PBIP* started in 1955 as a paperbound quarterly; the first issue listed 4,000 titles. It is now a hardbound annual, thicker than the thickest metropolitan telephone directory, with semiannual paperbound supplements.

Economically, a real Paperback Parnassus store would fail. Conceptually, it would be superfluous. Paperback publishing reaches an infinity of markets, and no one store could ever service them all. "Mass market" is the phrase used to describe an important class of paperbacks. But the phrase is misleading if it suggests that there is *one* mass market. There are many, both the mass kind and those of a more discrete character. It is the publisher's task, not always performed with certainty, to find the right ones for each individual paperback book.

Chapter
2
Two Paperback Worlds: Mass Market and Trade

While a tyro browser probably would not be aware of the distinction, the 123,000 items stocked at the Paperback Parnassus store divide basically into two types: "mass market" (or "drug store" or "newsstand") paperbacks; and "trade" (or "quality" or "bookstore") paperbacks. The distinction derives in part from the appearance of the books and in part from book publishing history. It is dictated primarily by the convenience of the book publishing industry in maintaining its own statistics. Otherwise, the significance of this distinction is of steadily declining importance.

There are, however, some general guidelines for identifying the two types of books.

Characteristics of a mass market paperback include the page size (usually 4¼″ x 7″), the price (anywhere from 75 cents to more than $2.25), the cover art (a poster approach, ranging from jazzy to barely concealed suggestiveness to frank titillation) and sales hype (flattering quotes, on front and back covers and first pages, from "big-name" authors and/or from reviews of the hardcover edition that have already appeared in

7

well-known newspapers and magazines). In conception, the book is a package designed to "jump off the rack," not unlike the popular magazines that may be on display in an adjacent department at the store.

A trade paperback's appeal is likely to be more subtle. Cover art will be more restrained, and there may be no cover art at all: just the author's name and the title, in austere type. Endorsement quotations, if any, will be of a more literary or scholarly nature. Page size will be about 5¼″ x 8″. Price will be somewhere between $1.50 and $6.00 or more.

Trade paperback titles in the store will outnumber mass market titles by a wide margin.

Mass market paperbacks offer a delicatessen of such staples as books that were hardcover best sellers; self-help and other reference books; mysteries, Westerns, Gothics, romances and other "escape" fiction; tie-ins with films or popular TV programs or cartoon features.

Trade paperbacks offer, in a somewhat quieter way, a similarly eclectic banquet, though a preponderance of the offerings seem to be keyed to the Groves, or at least the Suburbs, of Academe. The liberal arts and the sciences are equally well represented. If a best selling author appears in trade paperback, he is likely to be an author who has become recognized as a "classic," or the book is apt to be one that was not a best seller when it first appeared and only later gained an "underground" reputation that subsequently surfaced.

Regarding the publishers' names on the books—to the extent that any book buyer pays much attention to publishers' names—on mass market paperbacks, many of the names are those associated with big magazines and big communications companies (Fawcett, Dell, Warner, etc.). Those on trade paperbacks are mostly names familiar to readers of book review publications and literary and scholarly journals (Doubleday, Abrams, Viking, etc., and many university presses).

Two Paperback Worlds: Mass Market and Trade

In reality, of course, none of these distinctions means very much, and our Paperback Parnassus browser cannot be faulted for being blissfully unaware of them. Mass market paperback publishers, along with their traditional "pocket-size" books, have published both mini-sized (especially true in the children's book field) and maxi-sized (as big as the biggest slick magazines).

Trade paperback firms have published books that were hardcover best sellers, in part because author and publisher believed that trade paperbacking would give the book a longer life than it would have in the mass market. A book may have three lives: hardcover, trade paperback, and mass market paperback. Each edition reaches a different, although somewhat overlapping, audience.

Mass market publishers have produced books which, to all outward appearances, are trade paperbacks. Hardcover trade publishers have issued mass-market-looking paperback reprints of some of their books, which did not reach the usual mass market channels but which the publisher wants to keep in print and which he hopes will reach a new audience.

Trade paperback publishers are becoming more poster-oriented in their cover art. Mass market publishers' art directors, while still looking for covers that will make a book "jump off the rack," are becoming increasingly subtle in their competition with other publishers for rack space.

Perhaps the major factor that distinguishes trade paperbacks from mass market paperbacks is the way in which each type of book is distributed, although this distinction is not total. The modern mass market paperback, almost from its beginning, traveled the distribution routes pioneered by magazines and national newspapers. The modern trade paperback, from the start, was designed to sell in traditional book trade outlets, although with special emphasis on college bookstores. With the passage of time, however, each type of paperback has strayed into the other's distribution conduits.

Not all paperbacks, either mass market or trade, are destined for bookstores exclusively. Public, school, and college libraries, after years of scorning paperbacks because physically they were too fragile to survive multiple circulations, have begun to accept them, although most libraries do not bother to catalog them but, instead, make them available for unsupervised borrowing.

Classroom paperback book clubs, where students bring in their coins and teachers collect and forward them, represent yet another major outlet for paperbacks. Scholastic Magazines, Inc., pioneer in the classroom book club field, in 1974 distributed some 55 million paperbacks through its five clubs graded from kindergarten through grade 12. A key element in the success of such book clubs is that the children themselves select the books they get.

The book publishing industry itself has met these seeming anomalies of type of book and market by largely ignoring them. The Association of American Publishers, in compiling industry production statistics, basically looks not at individual books but at the firms which produced them. In the AAP's compilations, a trade paperback issued by a mass market firm is likely to be counted as a mass market book; a mass-looking and mass-priced paperback from a trade publisher is, despite appearance and price, regarded as a trade paperback. Adding to the statistical confusion: Some mass market publishers have trade publishing divisions; some trade publishers have mass market divisions; and some publishers work in all three areas of hardcover books, trade paperbacks and mass market paperbacks. Most of this multi-faceted output is correctly assigned in the AAP's periodic counts, but not all of it.

The result may be a statistician's nightmare. But it is also, in the variety of books offered, a reader's delight. A book is a book is a book, no matter how it gets to the reader.

Chapter
3
How the Books Arrive

Paperback Parnassus, as a large bookstore, has a considerable choice of simultaneously available sources from which it can order paperbacks. (As we shall see, such a choice of sources is not generally available to a much smaller store.)

For trade paperbacks, Parnassus can order either directly from publishers or from one or more jobbers.

For mass market paperbacks, it can order either directly from publishers or from one or more jobbers or from a local independent wholesaler (ID) or perhaps from an ID which is more distant geographically but which is interested in servicing the city where Parnassus is located.

In the world of paperbacks, and especially in the world of mass market paperbacks, the terms *jobber* and *independent wholesaler* have their own specific meanings. Added to them is the term *national distributor,* yet another link in the distribution chain.

National Distributors. There are about a dozen national distributors engaged in mass market paperback distribution.

Most of them started as corporate relatives of magazine publishers and they were either owned outright or were cooperatives established by a group of publishers—subsequently adding paperback representation. Some, through conglomeratization or other corporate change, are no longer owned by magazine publishers. Some act as financial backers of new magazines. At least one national distributor in this field handles books only. Some national distributors handle only books and magazines published by the distributors' owners; others distribute "outsiders'" books and magazines on a contract basis. National distributors have their own national sales forces; some also supplement their publisher-clients' promotion and publicity efforts with their own personnel in these areas. Some take almost all of their publishers' paperback output and service almost all markets. Others take only a percentage of their publishers' paperback output and concentrate on several markets only. Whatever their mix of product and market, the national distributors' most conspicuous contribution is as a conduit between publisher(s) and independent wholesalers.

Independent Wholesalers (IDs). There are more than 500 IDs in the U.S. and Canada. Although not all of these are significant for paperbacks, some 95 percent of the IDs handle at least some paperbacks. Most IDs started as locally-owned local distributors of magazines and national newspapers. Later, paperbacks were added to the mix. One characteristic of an ID is that it handles magazines. A second characteristic is that an ID places prime reliance on its own truck fleet for distribution. An ID buys most of its magazines at a discount of 40 percent off cover price and delivers them to retailers at a discount of 20 percent. An ID buys paperbacks at a discount of up to 46 percent and sells them to retailers at discounts of from 20 percent to 36 percent. Sales incentive programs may increase these discounts, and the whole discount structure is constantly negotiable. An ID operates as a *de facto* or *de jure* franchise in a fixed geographical area (usually a city and surrounding counties). The franchise is exclusive to the extent that other IDs usually are unlikely to invade the territory. Invasion has taken place in some areas as a result of a retail chain's insistence on having a single book source for all of its stores, regardless of their locations. The franchise is non-exclusive to the extent that publishers and jobbers are not prohibited from supplying direct service to accounts in the ID's area. Local ownership continues to characterize IDs, although there are a number of multi-agency ownerships and at least one conglomerate that owns a number of IDs. Some IDs have their own book and magazine retail stores. Some IDs also operate as jobbers.

Jobbers. In the mass market paperback field, a characteristic of a jobber is that it does not handle magazines. A second characteristic is that a jobber is not confined to a geographical area. A third characteristic is that a jobber does not place prime reliance on its own trucks for distribution; it mainly relies on the Post Office, United Parcel Service and common carriers.

As between mass market and trade paperbacks, these channels are not entirely distinct. Some IDs, while geared to the mass sale of national newspapers and magazines and paperbacks, have added trade paperbacks and even some hardcover books, primarily to service local schools and, to a lesser extent, trade bookstores. Some jobbers, traditionally handling hardcover books and trade paperbacks, have added lines of mass market paperbacks.

The ID is a key element, unique to the U.S. and Canada, in the modern paperback story. The modern mass market paperback "revolution" became possible not because it offered paper bindings and low retail prices, but because it employed techniques of mass production (most notably the introduction of the high-speed rubber plate rotary press) and mass distribution, in which the IDs are an essential, if now somewhat problematic, link.

Chapter
4

Distribution Comes of Age, or Atrophy

Historically, the ID is a descendant of the news butchers who met the trains in the late 1800s to peddle magazines and national newspapers. According to contemporary accounts, these entrepreneurs were a raffish lot. Territorial rights to a particularly desirable depot or street corner were often established through fistfights or even more violent expressions of the free enterprise spirit. This cut-and-shoot approach has characterized periodical distribution at various times and in various forms throughout its history and is not very far beneath the surface of the industry today. Present brigandage may be more sophisticated than its predecessors, but it is part of a ripe tradition.

By 1900, the American News Company (ANC) had a virtual monopoly on magazine and national newspaper distribution. One area in which the company was not active involved "tip" sheets and other racing publications, appendages of the race track wire services which helped meet the oft-felt needs of bookies, gamblers and like-minded venture capitalists. Local freebooters handled the race track publications. "Independent," in their context, meant independent of the American News Company.

15

In the early decades of the 20th century, these independents moved beyond race track publications and began to
challenge ANC's monopoly in magazines and national
newspapers. They were aided by a number of national
newspaper and magazine publishers which, in the interest of
maximizing sales, helped establish local wholesalers by
virtually giving them the franchise to compete with
local ANC branches. Not surprisingly, in view of the
independents' ancestral connection with the race track
tenderloin, a number of these competitive situations drew the
interest of fringes of the local criminal underworld, as
newspaper circulation wars erupted in many cities in the 1920s.
Several senior citizens in the ID community, now in honored
retirement, started their careers by driving delivery trucks with
shotguns under the front seats.

Through the 1930s and the World War II years, however, the
News Company dominated national magazine distribution
and was an important factor in the distribution of hardcover
books. When the new firm of Pocket Books started the modern
mass market paperback "revolution" in 1939, with the
intention of putting prime reliance on magazine distribution
channels, it sold to both the News Company and the
independents and directly to retail stores as well. So did most
of the other paperback companies that started in the years
immediately afterward. There was, after all, no reason to
change existing patterns. During the war, a publisher could sell
practically anything he could print to the well-heeled civilian
population or to the various government and private agencies
that were supplying books and magazines to the servicemen.

But following the war, paperback wholesaling became an
"either/or" franchise proposition: either a publisher dealt with
the News Company or, via a national distributor, with the IDs.
Pocket Books, New American Library and Bantam Books
were with the IDs. Dell and Popular Library were with the
News Company. In utilizing IDs as in so much else, Pocket
Books was the pioneer. One day in 1940, Wallis E. Howe, Jr.,

16

Pocket Books' first sales manager, stopped in a bar in Denver. The man on the next stool turned out to be Joe Morton, manager of the Rocky Mountain News Company, and as the talk got going it developed that Mr. Howe had a product which Mr. Morton could use. Newspaper and magazine wholesalers are a gregarious lot and talk among themselves freely. News of Mr. Morton's success with Pocket Books in Denver spread, and within a very few years Pocket Books had more than 600 independent wholesalers across the country distributing its product through some 100,000 newsstands, bookstores, stationery stores, food stores and other points of sale.

Success of this kind made the thought of an alternative to the American News Company, in an "either/or" situation, palatable. In 1945, the News Company had some 400 branches (warehouses) in the U.S. and Canada. Ten years later, it was down to 35 branches, and its paperback and magazine division was reported to be losing money. Anticipating the closing of the division, Dell, Popular Library and the many magazines that had distributed through ANC shifted to independent distribution, and the ANC publications division indeed was terminated in 1957. Members of the Council for Independent Distribution (CID), formed in 1955 as a trade association of IDs, were now as much a monopoly as the old News Company had been. Every paperback publisher was now tied, either by contract or through ownership, with a major national distributor, usually one whose principal traffic was in magazines. The publishers continued to service some accounts directly, of course. In the 1940s and 1950s, variety chains such as Woolworth and Kresge developed as important direct accounts, although they later would pose problems to their sources of supply.

At the local level, ANC's withdrawal from paperback and magazine distribution seemed to have put the IDs in a very strong position, and so it was for a while. But starting in the late 1950s, their market share was threatened by at least two new phenomena.

17

The first was the paperback jobber, which typically started with the new trade paperbacks, the products of the second paperback "revolution," sold them to college and general bookstores, and then selectively added mass market paperback lines. Recognizing no geographical restrictions, the jobbers were free to roam the country, offering their services to accounts which might be dissatisfied with their local IDs and to discount-hungry chains that might desire central purchasing and/or billing. These jobbers were later joined in this function by some established hardcover book wholesalers that added mass market paperbacks to their inventories.

The second threat to the IDs was the rapid national growth of several well-financed bookstore chains, which bought their paperbacks directly from publishers; mainly because of their buying power, they received better discounts that way.

Seeking to hold their market share, the IDs moved in several ways. First, many opened their own stores, and there are now some 600 of these stores, most of them well appointed, well stocked, and well managed. All 600, if under one ownership, would constitute the largest bookstore chain in the country.

Second, IDs started an education campaign to promote to chain food and drug stores the idea that they should go beyond token or checkout-only representation of publications and establish Family Reading Centers of books and magazines. A key argument in this campaign was that such reading centers would bring the stores a return on investment of at least 375 percent. In 1975, the Council for Periodical Distributors Associations (CPDA), the trade association of IDs (and successor to CID), reported that as a result of this campaign, approximately 10,000 Family Reading Centers had been placed, averaging 19½ linear feet of rack space per installation, including an average of six feet for paperbacks. This adds up, according to CPDA, to approximately 960,000 pockets and represents $6.5 million in paperback inventory that was not in chain stores before the campaign started. Based on an annual

18

inventory turnover of ten, this is $65 million worth (at retail) of new business. An interesting by-product of these two developments has been the IDs' acceptance of the odd-sized (i.e., non-pocket-sized) mass market paperback book. The IDs saw that such books were selling in their own stores and in the Family Reading Centers they were servicing, and they began promoting them to their other accounts as well.

Third, some IDs became jobbers as well.

Fourth, some IDs moved beyond their established geographical areas and established branches in other areas they thought were poorly serviced.

Fifth, some IDs, having acquired chain store accounts in distant cities, moved to acquire other accounts in those cities, trying to gain the additional volume of business that would justify providing long-range service. They did this without the formalities of opening up branches or calling themselves jobbers. They moved into direct competition, by offering better discounts, with the local IDs who were on the scene. The potential for chaos in such a situation, with perhaps several IDs competing with each other in the same territory, is considerable and harks back to an earlier, gaudier era in ID history.

For the present, however, the results of all this self-improvement by IDs have been mostly salutary. True, the number of points of sale for mass market paperbacks is down: from an estimated 110,000 in 1960 to an estimated 60,000 to 80,000 in 1975. The demise of mom-and-pop stores is responsible for much of that decrease. But there are more pockets in more good bookstores—both the chains' and the IDs'—than there were before.

Wholesalers are regaining some of the business they lost to publishers, because some retailers have rediscovered the convenience of local sources of supply. But this gain for IDs has been offset somewhat by publishers' increased eagerness to take away IDs' key accounts and put them on a direct basis.

Some retailers now have more sources for mass market paperbacks than they had before; an individual store might be dealing with publishers directly, with a couple of jobbers, with the local ID or with a more distant ID which is hungry for new business. Since retailers and wholesalers can return unsold paperbacks for credit, a complicating aspect of this multiplicity of sources lies in the sorting of returns: Which unsold books came from where? A related complication is the relaxation of credit controls on shaky retailers: a slow-paying retailer, who may not yet have been put on a "hold" credit basis by his ID but who expects that such a "hold" is close at hand, now has new opportunities to open up new sources of credit.

The number of IDs handling books has declined, through consolidations. Of the approximately 500 in the U.S. and Canada, perhaps 200 are significant for paperback sales.

The ID field has at least one conglomerate. ARA Services, Inc., a New York Stock Exchange firm with head offices in Los Angeles, bought the District News Company, Washington, D.C., in 1968. ARA's principal businesses are in vending machines and in industrial and school feeding. But the company obviously saw a future in periodical distribution, for in rapid succession it acquired IDs in Milwaukee, Norfolk, Hawaii, Los Angeles, San Francisco, San Pedro (since sold), San Diego, Burbank, Oklahoma City, Houston (since sold), Albuquerque, and other cities, for a total of about 22. According to Standard & Poors (September 16, 1974), publication distribution (books and magazines) accounted for 13 percent of ARA's 1972-73 fiscal year revenues of $991,800,000. Industry sources estimate that ARA-owned agencies account for about 25 percent of the magazine distribution in the country. The percentage for paperbacks is probably smaller; publishers' estimates are that it is in the range of 10-15 percent of ID-distributed books.

The ARA situation attracted the attention of the Federal Trade Commission. The company consented to an FTC order to divest itself, effective March 21, 1974, of agencies with a total volume of approximately $6,900,000 (about 5 percent of the company's total publication volume), and to refrain from acquiring additional publication agencies for ten years if 25 percent or more of the proposed acquisition's business is in reshipping, or if the agency proposed to be acquired operates in California, Hawaii, the District of Columbia or Oklahoma.

Some attorneys close to book publishing expressed concern privately that a distributor as large as the ARA group could force tie-in sales of books and magazines on booksellers who wanted only books, but that was not a real issue in the FTC action. Instead, the FTC found that ARA's agency business had just spread too widely.

Nevertheless, a widespread, well-financed distribution firm such as ARA could in the future pose a threat both to competition in the field and to the unimpeded circulation of publications. Periodical distribution in the U.S. is already monopolistic to the extent that IDs have near-exclusives in the territories they service. But a group of IDs under one ownership, like the ARA group, could represent a real monopoly threat.

Particularly in the magazine field, some publishers privately have expressed concern that a major distribution group could use its strength to force greater discounts directly from publishers, using the threat that non-complying publishers would be shut out of several major markets simultaneously. In any such confrontation, paperbacks probably would be innocent victims, since agencies make less profit on books than they do on magazines. At agencies where management's sole concern is to maximize profits, the book departments might be terminated or at least sharply curtailed.

Many publishers are dissatisfied with the ID system, which now handles more than half of mass market paperbacks sold. The system accounts for tremendous waste, though assigning blame for this waste—whether it is the publishers' or the wholesalers' fault—is probably a moot point. The waste takes the form of IDs' returns of unsold books. A returned paperback, unlike a returned hardcover book, usually has no value.

Major paperback publishers have said, in public statements, that they allow the biggest and/or most successful IDs to set the quantities the IDs think they need. That is, for each new title or new reissue, the major publishers, on the basis of past sales histories, suggest how many copies each big, successful ID ought to take from the first printing. The big, successful IDs are free to accept, raise or lower their "suggested allotments." A lot of conversation may take place between the ID's book buyer and the publisher's or national distributor's salesman, but the final decision rests with the ID. Major publishers have said that they have the vast majority of IDs on this "suggested allotment" system. The rest of the IDs, small agencies which do little with books (as few as 10 percent, say many publishers), are force-fed the quantities the publishers think they should have.

This cooperative pose struck by the publishers might be convincing if it were not for two factors. First, some publishers have acknowledged that they inflate "suggested allotments" by as much as 25 percent, anticipating the cuts the IDs' buyers will make, in order to get the pre-set quantities required into the market. Second, an AAP survey of nine mass market publishers found that of $89 million worth of new releases shipped to U.S. and Canadian wholesalers in 1973, $85.5 million were shipped as "automatic," and only $4.5 million as "order only." "Automatic" may mean different things to different publishers, but the implication is clear: publishers remain free to force-feed the market. Publishers' posturing about IDs' buying independence is more than just public relations at industry conventions. It is reflective of a major conflict, in the industry's thinking, between traditional methods, which held that books would sell just because they were in the marketplace, and new approaches, which hold that the market must be courted and not just glutted.

Force-feeding has glutted the market in the past and continues to do so. The results have been wild over-production of books, a very short shelf life for those releases that get out of the warehouses and into the stores at all, tough competition for space in the limited number of pockets in stores, and the Big Shredder.

Chapter
5
The Anatomy of Waste

An ID returns unsold paperbacks by ripping off the covers and sending them back to the publisher for credit. (Sometimes, at the publisher's request, the ID will return whole books which the publisher believes are salable elsewhere, with the publisher paying the transportation charges.) Some IDs rip off the covers manually. Others, who can afford it, use an automatic stripping machine, which typically is available to an ID on a lease basis. It takes the covers off at one end and puts the denuded books into a shredder. Out the other end comes confetti. For one who loves books, it is a painful sight.

It is not unknown for an inefficient ID to be shredding a release in the back room while up in the office the book manager is reordering the same title. It is not unheard of for an ID with a cash flow problem to use covers of still active titles to pay his bills with publishers.

A publisher, reading his latest sales figures on the print-out from his IBM machine, must despair when he sees case after case of agencies which place good initial orders, solid reorders, and then return a quantity equal to the reorder plus. (He might

25

reflect that he himself had a heavy hand in setting the initial order, but probably he will not think about that.) Why, he will ask himself, did the ID bother to reorder at all? Because the ID didn't know what was going on in accounts in his own back yard? Some publishers tell their salesmen to check an ID's back room before they take reorders, but this tactic has been only sporadically successful.

IDs account for well over half of the mass market paperbacks shipped to all channels. They also account for a big percentage of the returns. A 1973 AAP survey of nine mass market publishers found that IDs received $202.3 million of the $320.2 million worth of books shipped to all channels, and IDs accounted for $89.9 million of the $112.9 million worth of books returned for credit. Also for 1973, a CPDA survey found that for 77 representative IDs, 54.6 percent of the books shipped to IDs were sold, and 45.4 percent were returned. When other types of accounts, which do not have the stripped-cover-only returns privilege but must return (and pay shipping charges for) full books, are added to the ID volume, the mass market paperback industry's returns percentage drops; but in 1973, the percentage was still an alarming 35.8 percent, with a range per company of from 24.2 percent to 49.5 percent.

Some publishers, surveying the waste in the ID system, have predicted a rapid end to the system, with all business going either directly to retailers or directly to jobbers. Some seem to be trying to hasten the system's end by taking major accounts away from IDs and putting them on a direct basis. But it is difficult to see how the mass market paperback, conceived for mass distribution, could continue in its present form and economics without the network of 500 IDs that can quickly get books into the pockets at 60,000 or more stores around the country. The great strength of the ID system is best seen in the way that books of a "hot news" and thus highly perishable nature are rushed to sale practically overnight. The great weakness of the ID system is best seen in the Big Shredder.

The existence of the shredding system has given rise to two curious illegal phenomena: covers that never had books and books that no longer have covers. It does not take genius but only an agreeable printer and a tap into the ID system in order to reproduce a paperback cover exactly, including any inventory code marks on the inside of the cover, and ship it to the publisher for credit. There are no mechanical systems now in use by publishers which can detect such counterfeits. Detection will come only when the publisher realizes—and this realization can take months—that certain agencies are returning covers in a quantity greater than the number of books they were shipped. The counterfeiter can minimize the risk of detection even more if he has access to a number of agencies through which he can feed his bogus covers. Fake covers do not pose a major ongoing problem in the paperback industry, but it is a problem that crops up periodically and probably will continue to do so.

Coverless books show up more frequently and in greater quantities in the marketplace, though the nature of this problem, too, is sporadic. Basically, it is the ID's responsibility to certify, whether by affidavit or on some kind of honor system, that he has destroyed the books whose covers he is returning for credit. He may destroy them with machinery in his own warehouse, or he may sell them to a wastepaper dealer who says that *he* will destroy them. Either way, the possible sources of slippage are many. Stripped books could be "detoured" on their way to the shredder by IDs, jobbers, retailers, printers, wastepaper dealers or disgruntled employees of any of them. One way the traffic operates may be seen in an incident in the spring of 1975 at an Ohio ID's warehouse: employees there found crudely printed fliers, under the windshield wipers of their cars in the company parking lot, from an Indiana firm offering to buy stripped books and magazines.

An important decision on the stripped books business was issued in June 1975 by the New York State Supreme Court, which held that the only permissible resale of stripped paperbacks is for the purpose of destroying the stripped books. The plaintiff in the case was an upstate New York firm which dealt primarily in remaindered hardcover books but which also offered retailers assortments of stripped paperbacks at $80 per 1000 books. Simon & Schuster, the publisher that initiated the lawsuit in 1971, reguires IDs and other accounts with the cover returns privilege to sign "certificates of destruction," stating that they have indeed destroyed the books on which they are claiming credit. But in a ruling midway through the action, Justice Irving H. Saypol held that whether or not such assurances are required in writing, it is a breach of trade practice—and therefore of a vendor's responsibility—to sell stripped books to another for resale as books. He recognized the validity of the trade practice as a means of reducing distribution costs, thus permitting lower retail prices, and as protection for "legitimate wholesalers and retailers" and copyright owners "against bootleggers." While the decision applies only to Simon & Schuster books and, technically, only to New York State (although the defendant company had shipped stripped paperbacks across state lines), it is likely to have a chilling effect on the stripped paperback trade, at least temporarily.

While publishers may bemoan the waste in the ID system, they bear a major responsibility for it. In an average month, an ID receives about 350 releases—new titles and reissues—and that is more than most of them can handle. Reliance on "suggested allotment" systems has not ameliorated that fact. Yet publishers show no sign of exercising any birth control on title production. CPDA found that in 1974, IDs received 4254 releases, compared to 4643 in 1973. The 389-title decline was almost wholly attributable to book lines that went inactive or totally out of business in 1974—which may be the only way to accomplish a decrease in production. At the same time, however, there is a universal complaint that the number of titles is increasing faster than the number of available pockets in stores, thus reducing an individual book's shelf life.

The shelf life of a paperback, assuming it gets out of the ID's warehouse at all, can be as short as a week. Or, in the case of a hardy perennial like Dr. Spock, shelf life can be relatively forever. (A corollary problem is the book whose shelf life is, in terms of sales, too long: the book that just sits there in its pocket, month after month. This situation is most likely to occur in stores where the management cares little about such necessary business considerations as inventory turnover. Fortunately, such book departments are rare and are not likely to stay in business very long.)

A key figure in determining a book's shelf life is an ID's truck driver as he makes his rounds of the stores he services. He brings the new releases into a store, pulls some of the old ones and puts the new ones in. He may do this with skill; indeed, he may know more than anyone about what a neighborhood is reading and what it wants to read; if he works for an ID which has an incentive program for its drivers, the rewards of his expertise can be tangible. Or he may do it like an automaton: so many Westerns in, so many out; so many mysteries in, so many out. Watch out, Dr. Spock! IDs may not want to be force-fed by publishers, but they force-feed the majority of their outlets; and many store managers are happy with that arrangement, for it spares them a kind of thinking that they are not really prepared to do.

The key position held by the truck driver is the subject of much despondent head-shaking by publishers, perhaps because they have never ridden with a skillful routeman (or perhaps because they have ridden only with inept ones). Or perhaps because they have never ridden an ID's truck at all.

Some of the industry's deeper thinkers are convinced that decision making about the life of a book can no longer be left to truck drivers. For example, the Charles Levy agency in

Chicago, an acknowledged giant in the ID field, has devised a system of computer cards to be inserted in each pocket in a store and to regulate the reorder-or-pull problem. It has applied the system to its jobber operation, Computer Book Service, and has plans to apply it to its ID operation as well.

Since 1973, CPDA has been promoting the application of the Universal Product Code (UPC) to books and magazines. UPC is those little gray lines of varying width and length and with accompanying numbers that one sees on most nationally marketed food products, such as Nabisco cookies. With UPC, a checkout clerk, using a scanner wand connected to a computer, can record a sale, note it for inventory purposes and provide other input such as demographics. Food stores are using it; variety chains and big department stores are testing it. The time is not far off when major supermarket chains will make buying decisions based on whether a product carries UPC markings. The first magazines to carry UPC markings were *Family Circle* and *Women's Day,* with their February 1975 issues.

Paperback publishers are not exactly delighted at the UPC prospect. Those little UPC lines, not very attractive, would probably have to go on the covers of books, a thought that may send publishers' art directors out on strike. Some publishers say that food chains represent less than 5 percent of the paperback market and therefore are not worth the extra effort. Some say they will comply if the supermarkets insist on UPC. Some argue that it is up to the chains' managers to determine whether books are sufficiently profitable for them to handle books on a non-UPC basis. All agree that CPDA is unduly alarmist and that UPC is years away as far as books are concerned. CPDA, in reply, notes that the UPC now involves stores with a total of some 100,000 paperback pockets.

The Levy system, UPC or some similar computer-based program offers hope for greater efficiency to an industry not noted for it. Such a system could tell a computer-equipped ID what he is selling where and maybe enable him to avoid unnecessary returns; instead, he could clean up copies returned from one store and send them to another in a different part of town where the demographics are different.

For publishers, such a system could provide input for a centralized market research data bank. Each major publisher, with his own electronic data processing, thinks he knows what he has going for himself in the marketplace. But no one knows very specifically what is going on in the marketplace as a whole.

Among most publishers and IDs alike, there is considerable reluctance to join the world of the computer more fully. Most IDs feel that they do not do a large enough business in books and periodicals to justify an investment in electronic data processing equipment. And in a business which traditionally has been people-intensive, there is a natural hesitancy about turning major decision making over to machines.

There has been little cooperative market research among mass market paperback publishers primarily because the publishers are so fiercely competitive. Also, in the past, federal agencies at times have tarred the whole paperback industry with a broad brush—on issues such as allegedly smutty covers, allegedly deceptive retitling of older books, "promotion allowances" alleged to be little more than kickbacks to big retailers—and this may have made the publishers gun-shy of any situation where cooperation could allegedly be "collusion." IDs can talk to each other because territorially they are basically exclusive, goes this line of reasoning, but publishers cannot.

But if the mass market is fragmenting the way it seems to be, and if the industry is not going to drown in a sea of unsold books, some sort of cooperative market research by publishers, national distributors, IDs, retailers and their various trade associations will become increasingly necessary.

Chapter
6
IDs: A Composite Portrait

The 500 or more IDs in the U.S. and Canada have a variety of shapes and sizes, depending in large measure on the shapes and sizes of the markets they serve. In the way they handle the distribution of books, they range from indifferent to excellent.

That range may reflect the quality of the markets the ID services, or (less likely) the nature of the ID's service may affect the quality of its markets. Certainly, a territory with a number of colleges and universities, good public school systems, a substantial increment of white-collar industry and an above-average per capita income offers an ID more attractive demographics than a territory that is educationally impoverished and dominated by heavy industry and/or agriculture.

A medium-sized ID, above average in the quality of its service, would have gross sales of about $6 million, representing about $2 million in books, $3 million in magazines and $1 million in national newspapers. It would employ about 100 people. It would have a fleet of a dozen or more trucks, serving accounts in a metropolitan area and several adjacent counties. Of all its accounts, some 300 would be book accounts (some taking books along with magazines and newspapers and others taking books only), and these accounts would have an average of 250-300 pockets for paperbacks. These accounts would be visited by an agency truck driver once or twice a week (less frequently in the case of quite small accounts), and the driver would have a prime responsibility in determining which new titles go up on the racks, which titles get a supplementary distribution of more copies, and which titles have a long enough rack exposure and are to be removed. The driver may make this determination in consultation with members of the store's staff; or, with the store management's blanket approval, the driver may make the entire determination himself. If the store staff and the driver have a real "feel" for books and what is selling, the racking decisions will be made mostly on a book-by-book, title-by-title basis. If they don't, decision making will be a process which tends to depersonalize books: so many titles in each price range, so many in each subject category—up they go on the racks, and off they come.

A driver may cover 10-12 accounts each day. Or in the case of accounts requiring quite tailor-made service, justifying five or six hours of a driver's time, he may cover only one or two. The key consideration, as IDs have learned only recently, is the number of pockets, not the number of accounts, serviced.

It takes a minimum order of $80-$100 to make a driver's visit to an account worthwhile to an ID. The biggest accounts—some with 5000 pockets or more—will get copies of every single new release each month. Some will get assortments pre-packaged at the agency: category books, for example, or books old and new by a best-selling author. For the rest of the accounts, no effort is made to get all of a month's titles on display. What goes on the shelves there represents the collective wisdom, based on past performance of the accounts and the books and authors in question, of the agency's buyers, the driver, and sometimes store personnel.

This kind of decision making might lend itself to computerization. But computers are little in evidence in the ID field, perhaps because individualism in decision making is, for better or worse, a strong tradition among IDs. Computers are likely to be used only for billing accounts, and that function is likely to be farmed out to an independent data processing service.

Books may be delivered by IDs to stores either prepackaged, along with prepackaged magazine assortments, or separately from magazines in bookmobiles: trucks carrying only books, several thousand dollars worth per truck each day. Whichever method is used (some agencies use both), magazines are more important to agencies than books for at least three reasons—magazines represent a larger volume, afford better discounts and have continuity. The January issue of a monthly magazine will be followed by a February issue; but each book is a separate item, although some series and genre books and some best-selling authors do build up a sales continuum of readership.

Of late, however, some IDs have come to regard books as relatively more attractive. First, the mortality rate among big magazines has been high in recent years, and the death of a major magazine is reflected immediately in an ID's sales figures. Second, books offer IDs an avenue for expanding into educational markets; book fairs at schools and teachers' conferences are a small but growing activity for many IDs. Mainly because of school business, some IDs are now stocking some trade paperbacks and even some hardbacks as well.

Third, paperback bookstores—both those owned by IDs and those owned by others—have proved successful in many suburban locations as books have followed readers out the Interstate and into the shopping centers.

Fourth, many large retail chains have rediscovered IDs as convenient local sources for books and magazines, although in the economic recession of the mid-1970s, some chains have ordered their store managers to cut back inventories and have sent book suppliers edicts which are not always beneficial to book availability. These edicts put prime emphasis on best sellers, almost to the exclusion of other types of books, and have all but banned special publications and special display racks from the chains' stores. A reader in search of diversity would have to look elsewhere than in a chain store. The chains also have a disruptive impact on the ID structure when a chain, in the interest of getting centralized delivery and billing and better discounts, asks an ID to supply some or all of the chain's stores, regardless of location. If an ID wants a chain's business and agrees, he may find himself sending trucks considerable distances to service only a few stores—not an economically rewarding exercise. To make it more rewarding, the ID may try to pick up other accounts or even establish branch warehouses in these distant territories, thus poaching on the resident ID.

Among paperback publishers and national distributors, folklore has it that IDs are the "fat cats" along the distribution pipelines. While it is true that the executives of a successful ID can live very well, industry statistics dispute the thought that the ID link in the chain represents excessive added value. CPDA, in a 1973 operating survey covering 91 IDs, found that their net income, before federal taxes, as a percentage of net sales was 4.68 percent. (By way of slight contrast, an AAP survey of nine mass market publishers reported net income for 1973 before federal taxes averaging 6.2 percent of gross sales.)

The IDs' post-tax net income as a percentage of net sales was 2.95 percent, a decline from the 3.22 percent reported by 92 IDs in 1972. Gross profit as a percentage of net sales dropped from 24.10 percent in 1972 to 23.97 percent in 1973. Operating expenses as a percentage of net sales increased from 20.27 percent in 1972 to 20.51 percent in 1973.

Among CPDA's conclusions: "Dollar volume growth due to general cover price increases have for many become a substitute for real growth in unit sales and an ominous and misleading statistic on which to base the long-term growth of this industry."

IDs: A Composite Portrait

For purposes of the survey, CPDA divided IDs into four groups, based on sales volume: under $500,000; $500,000 to $1 million; $1-2 million; and over $2 million. The IDs in the smallest group were the most profitable, with average net income of 4.38 percent of net sales. The largest were the least profitable: 2.51 percent of net income. Such statistics might give an ID pause before he expands into a more full-time book operation. The smallest group, with the smallest inventory increase in 1973, showed a rate of inventory turnover of 37.82 times. The largest group, with the largest inventory increase, turned inventory over 11.59 times. The smallest group had returns from dealers of 32 percent of gross dealer sales; the largest group had returns of 39 percent. (Books and magazines are included in this survey. Overall sales mix was 29 percent books, 67 percent magazines, 4 percent children's books.)

A typical big/successful ID is likely to be a locally-owned, second generation business. (Although, as has already been noted, there are some multi-agency ownerships and at least one conglomerate in the field.) The agency was started by the father, who came up through the rough-and-tumble of the 1920s' circulation wars, and is now carried on by his son or son-in-law, who is usually a university graduate. The family more often than not is Jewish, or it might be Irish. The son or son-in-law is likely to be active in religious and community affairs, especially those relating to education.

Inside the agency's warehouse, activity on any given day may range from grim determination to frenzy, for each day the agency has a lot of publications to sort and load on trucks in time for the drivers to make their appointed rounds. The book department itself is jammed with books, including more older books than might once have been the case; a lot of the education business is backlist business. The arrangement of books will be rudimentary—by publishers' lines and, perhaps, by major subject categories. A more sophisticated arrangement is not needed, a visitor will be told, because the people who pick the books are experienced and know where to find the titles they need. No one can tell the visitor how many books are in inventory, because the agency does not count the books that way. But management can give a highly accurate estimate as to the dollar value of the books in inventory.

The warehouse will be an unhandsome building, with minimum human comforts, surrounded on at least two sides by sufficient asphalt to give incoming and outgoing trucks ample room to maneuver. It is likely to be surrounded by high wire fence, for it is in a run-down part of the city. Actually or symbolically, the warehouse is "down by the tracks," even though the trains may not run through anymore. "Down by the tracks" is where the IDs started. The business has come a long way since then, but the traditions have not entirely disappeared. Besides, whoever thought a book warehouse should be luxurious?

Chapter
7
What Future for Export?

American trade paperbacks and mass market paperbacks are sold in export in many of the same ways as are other kinds of American books. But as might be expected, the mass market books present some interesting wrinkles of their own, although there is nothing overseas comparable to the ID network that exists in the U.S. and Canada.

The export marketing situation for U.S. mass market paperbacks may be on the verge of some considerable change. Differences of opinion exist, within the industry and even within individual firms, about the shape that such change may be expected to take. The most vocal proponents of change emphasize that they are speaking as individuals—not for the industry (indeed, it is doubtful that anybody could speak for the highly competitive paperback industry) and sometimes not even for their own firms.

It is clear that today's export situation for U.S. mass market paperbacks is not what it was in the decade after World War II, when U.S. government overseas book programs were relatively more important than they are now and when U.S. paperbacks sold in overseas markets primarily just because the books were there. As is the case in the domestic market, more creative merchandising is required now to sell paperbacks abroad. Old ways of serving the various overseas markets are increasingly being questioned as obsolete.

For mass market paperbacks, as for almost all other types of American books, export represents a small part of total sales. The small size of the percentage raises a chicken-or-egg kind of question: Is the percentage for export small because publishers have paid relatively little attention to export, or is relatively little attention paid to export because the percentage is small? Some "young Turks" in the U.S. book trade and in other countries' book trades feel that American book export has languished because publishing management has treated it as a stepchild for too long.

An AAP survey found that in 1974, export markets, not including Canada, accounted for 4.5 percent of mass market paperback publishers' receipts and 5.4 percent of units sold. Industry estimates are that Canada accounted for another 9-13 percent. Returns of unsold copies, expressed as a percentage of gross sales (dollars), were 17.9 percent for the export market, compared to 35.1 percent for the U.S. and Canada.

Since 1974 was the first year for which AAP undertook this particular survey, the results cannot be taken entirely literally, even though the companies surveyed represent about 93 percent of the mass market paperback industry. As is especially true of most new statistical surveys, reporting procedures from one publishing house to another may be far from uniform. It is possible, for example, that some Canadian sales were included as "export," even though the participating publishers were specifically asked to exclude Canada from their reports. And it is not certain how many trade paperbacks are included in the totals, for many of the reporting publishers issue both mass market and trade softcover books.

What Future for Export?

The AAP figures do not include, and probably never could include, export paperback sales by domestic jobbers. U.S. government figures on book exports contain their own built-in limitations and offer little corrective help in determining the size of the paperback export market. Industry experts estimate that the AAP's 4.5 percent figure probably should be doubled in the interest of accuracy. That would mean an export total, in terms of publishers' receipts, of about $2.4 million in 1974 (not including Canada). Nobody knows for sure.

Some mass market paperback publishers farm out most of their export sales effort to one or another of the U.S.-based book sales representation firms that are active on a worldwide basis. At least one paperback firm has its own export distributor that is a part of its wholly-owned domestic national distributor, but it uses an independent American sales representative in certain secondary or tertiary foreign markets.

A big paperback house may use a three-pronged approach to foreign sales: (1) *primary markets*, such as the United Kingdom, a wholly-owned subsidiary, which takes the books of the U.S. parent firm whenever marketing rights are available and also engages in indigenous publishing; (2) *secondary markets,* such as the major countries of Western Europe, an independent local jobber, which has the exclusive right to sell the publisher's books in the territory the jobber covers; and (3) *tertiary markets,* an independent American export representative.

From the publisher's viewpoint, such a three-pronged approach has some interesting competitive aspects. For example, if an American independent sales representative brings a particular territory up to the point where it need no longer be considered tertiary, the publisher, in the interest of maximizing sales, may take it away from the independent American sales representative and assign it to a local jobber. The big American sales representatives try to counter such a possibility by establishing their own sales subsidiaries in such territories, which the sales representative does not regard

41

as tertiary because it represents a broad spectrum of American publishers there. It is impossible to generalize about the rights and wrongs of this issue of U.S. export sales representative vs. local jobber, for each territory is a special case. But the competition, real or potential, between the two channels should,when it is working properly, keep everyone involved on his toes and, indeed, help to maximize sales.

Mass market paperbacks are more exportable than other kinds of American books mainly because their cover prices are lower. But low price is no automatic guarantee of success in foreign markets. In markets where an American paperback title is in direct competition with a British paperback of the same title, the British edition will carry the lower price. If the U.S. edition has a cover price of $1.25, the British version will be priced at the equivalent of 75 or 80 cents. This price gap may narrow if the rate of inflation in the United Kingdom continues to outstrip the rate in the U.S. But that is no assurance of marketing parity. For most American mass market paperback publishers agree that their British counterparts do a far superior export marketing job because, among other reasons, exports for a British publisher represent a far greater percentage of total sales than they do for an American publisher. A British publisher is likely to think that exports, far from being peripheral, are essential to his survival.

Export best sellers among American mass market paperbacks are not very different from domestic best sellers, although the number of titles and the number of copies sold per title are smaller. Books that were best sellers in hardcover, books that are movie and TV tie-ins, "breakthrough" nonfiction books like *Future Shock* are in demand abroad as they are at home. A top mass market best seller in export would represent a sale of about 250,000 copies, and such books do not come along every year. A second category, good steady sellers in export, consists of mass market paperback editions of American classics that are still in copyright, such as books by Hemingway, Faulkner and Fitzgerald. "Average" books on an

What Future for Export?

American paperback publisher's list tend to get slighted abroad, for they receive no visible promotion or publicity support. Along with movie and television tie-ins, the most important hype for American paperbacks abroad is the best seller lists appearing in the international editions of *Time* and *Newsweek*.

With movie and television tie-ins of books in export, a continuous awareness of timing is essential, for films and TV series do not go public everywhere around the world at the same time. As of mid-1975, for example, Australia was holding off the *Star Trek* TV programs until its television systems developed color capability. This awareness of timing involves a close coordination among the export sales, the publicity and the rights departments in each house, and not all houses think that export is important enough to warrant the extra promotional effort. Once in a while, a promotion department will arrange a telephone interview between an author in the U.S. and a radio talk-show broadcaster abroad, but such extra effort does not happen often.

More often, this is the kind of thing that happens: A movie opens in a foreign country. It is a tremendous popular success, and the local distributor, unprepared or uninformed, is caught woefully short of copies of the tie-in book. For the publisher back in the U.S., facing the situation squarely, the alternatives are resignation about irretrievably lost sales or using air freight which, because of rising fuel costs, has become almost prohibitively expensive (up to 20 cents per paperback copy to Europe, up to $1 per copy to Japan).

In most overseas markets, most American paperback covers do not seem the lurid "come hithers" they seemed when U.S. paperbacks made their first international appearance after World War II. Such acceptance of U.S. covers may be because the recent covers themselves have been toned down, or it may be because the local product on the newsstands has equalled or even surpassed the American in its degree of titillation. British paperback publishers have been known to do special covers for

43

special export markets, such as a very plain, all-type cover for markets known to be especially straight-laced. With that in mind, some American paperback exporters have wondered aloud from time to time whether their books would sell better if their cover art took local *mores*, plus or minus, into account. But so far, it appears, export has not seemed sufficiently important to American paperback firms to encourage them to do tailor-made covers for their overseas customers.

Some of the factors that inhibit an all-out export push for American mass market paperbacks involve the British Traditional Market Rights Agreement. Under this agreement as it has operated in the past, an American originating publisher (usually hardcover), selling publishing and reprint licensing rights in a work of American authorship to a British publisher, has sold exclusive marketing rights in the British Commonwealth except Canada. The U.S. Department of Justice has explored the antitrust implications of this agreement, which is enforced by the British Publishers Association, and has worked out a cease-and-desist consent decree.

On September 24, 1975, members of the British Publishers Asscciation voted to discontinue the Market Rights Agreement, on condition that a significant number of the 21 U.S. publisher-defendants reach an antitrust agreement with the Justice Department. If such agreements are reached, the prospect is that territories hitherto regarded as part of the British Commonwealth for rights purposes will be openly negotiable for publishing rights on a book-by-book basis.

The basic conflict is between those who desire wide-open international marketing and those who insist on the letter and spirit of the Universal Copyright Convention, which permits copyright owners to assign rights by territory. While this conflict has yet to be resolved, the long-term prospect is for more open marketing opportunities for both U.S. and British publishers. Meanwhile, the British agreement still applies to major markets such as Australia, New Zealand and South Africa—though basically not to Canada, which because of geography is a special case.

Paperbacks are involved more than other kinds of books with the impact of the Traditional Market Rights Agreement. The agreement's effect may be seen sharply in the case of an American book which (1) becomes a hardcover best seller; (2) whose Commonwealth rights—hardcover *and* paperback— have been sold to a London publisher; and (3) which comes out, six months or a year after U.S. hardcover publication, as a U.S. paperback.

London publishers tend to be much slower than their American colleagues about letting a book go into paperback. As a result, booksellers and readers in Australia, New Zealand, South Africa and other Commonwealth outposts are denied by the letter of the Traditional Market Rights Agreement, for months or years or perhaps forever, inexpensive copies of that book they have seen reviewed or on the best seller lists in international *Time* and *Newsweek*. In reality, of course, they are not always denied, for Commonwealth booksellers frequently have winked at the letter of the agreement and bought the books directly from U.S. jobbers. But such "buying around" does not make for a tidy situation.

"Young Turks" in the Australian book trade have vocally challenged the Traditional Market Rights Agreement, and no doubt their counterparts in the New Zealand and South African book trades are watching for the results. Among U.S. paperback publishers, those most in support of Australia's "young Turks" have been those which have no London subsidiaries and would love to sell their paperbacks directly to the Commonwealth Market. To the extent that these firms are publishing more original books, they are freer to do so, of course, but they have not been challenging the Rights Agreement, at least not publicly.

45

On the other hand, U.S. paperback publishers which have investments in United Kingdom subsidiaries have been less eager to upset established applecarts, for fear that the loss of Commonwealth markets might make the U.K. subsidiaries economically unviable. Some say, too, that they fear that open market status for Australia might actually harm the Australian book trade, since at least in theory, Australia might have two paperback editions of every new book—one from the U.S., one from the U.K.—instead of one—from the U.K., as matters now stand; thus, the market would be glutted and indigenous publishing might be discouraged as well. Self-determination is the answer, say Australia's "young Turks." Meanwhile, Australia's booksellers continue to buy around.

The marketing rights controversy, as epitomized by Australia, is not unique to the English-speaking world as far as philosophical conflicts are concerned. Portugese publishers are trying to keep Brazil as a captive market in the face of Brazilian publishers who frequently can outbid them for rights. Similarly, in the rest of Latin America, Spanish publishers are trying to hold the line against well-funded, ambitious local publishers. It is not just a case of London vs. New York. It is the old ways of publishing books vs. the new, whatever these new ways ultimately turn out to be.

For the present, the international market for American paperbacks is three-part: the British Commonwealth, Canada, and the open market, which is basically the rest of the world. As noted above, Canada is a special case and might best be described as a "closed open market." With English-language books in paperback, Canada is likely to get the U.S. edition if the author is American, the United Kingdom edition if the author is British, and the edition of whoever first published the book and licensed the paperback if the author is Canadian. (To the distress of the small Canadian publishing industry, Canadian authors, once they have achieved a degree of success, tend to send their manuscripts to New York or London and not to Toronto.) But this is not a hard-and-fast situation. Sometimes in Canada, U.S. and U.K. paperback editions are in direct competition. And, of course, Canadian booksellers "buy around" through U.S. and U.K. jobbers. (It is likely that Australia soon will become a second "closed open market," developing *de jure* into what is now becoming *de facto*.)

Though the Canadian book trade may not like it, most U.S. publishers regard Canada as an extension of the U.S. market. But especially for mass market publishers, because of the quantities involved, Canada is special, too, in that it is one of the few civilized countries that still charge duties on imported books. To avoid paying duties, and willy-nilly to help the Canadian printing industry, most U.S. mass market publishers for most of their titles ship films and not actual books to Canada, and the Canadian editions are produced there.

As mass market paperback publishers expand from their traditional base as reprinters and publish more and more originals, they are becoming more and more involved in the international publishing rights field. No one seems to know the dollar volume earned by these publishers in international rights sales, but no doubt it is growing. Here, too, there is some dissatisfaction with established ways of doing business. Some question whether the massive annual Frankfurt Book Fair in West Germany is valid as a rights fair in an age when international rights sales are initiated and consummated by international telephone and cable. Some would like to see a big international rights fair in the U.S., perhaps alternating with Frankfurt: the U.S. in even-numbered years, perhaps, and Frankfurt in odd-numbered years. Meanwhile, all continue to go to Frankfurt every year.

As people in the industry offer suggestions for change and think about timetables for change, perhaps this is enough to say for now: Paperback publishing over the years has developed in a series of breakthroughs into new ways of publishing and distributing books. The export arm of the paperback industry, while doing reasonably well these days, can hardly be considered immune to some future breakthroughs of its own.

Chapter
8
Birth, Life and Death in the Mass Market

A book comes into being basically because an editor believes that the project is economically viable and/or will make a contribution to knowledge and because he is able to convince his colleagues in the publishing house, especially the management, with his enthusiasm. This is true for both hardcover and paperback books. But with paperbacks, there are some differences.

A major difference stems from the fact that paperbacking is still heavily dependent on reprinting books that first appeared in hardcover. Paperback originals continue to grow in number, but they are not yet a dominant factor in the industry's total output.

So, an editor in a paperback house is apt to be looking principally for books that he can reprint. He will be looking for books that have done well in hardcover. With each prospective candidate for reprinting, he will be asking himself questions such as: Did the book in hardcover make any of the various best seller lists? If so, how high did it get on the lists, and how many weeks did it stay there? Is it a book by an author who has done consistently well in paperback? (If it is,

49

the firm that published the author previously in paperback may have an inside track on his next paperback.) Does the book fall into one of the established categories that do well in the mass market, such as mysteries or Westerns or other "escape" fiction? Is a movie or television tie-in in the offing?

If the book is scheduled for hardcover publication but has not yet appeared and the paperback editor is making a judgment from manuscript or galley proofs, he will ask himself, in addition to the above questions and quite aside from the book's literary merit, such things as: How much is the hardcover publisher investing in the advertising, promotion and publicity for the book? Has the author or the hardcover publisher sold additional subsidiary rights, so that the book may be expected to get additional public exposure through excerpts or serialization in a big magazine or news service? Will the author be making appearances on radio and TV "talk" shows? If a movie version of the book is likely, will the film's producer put up some money to advertise and promote the book, thus enhancing the public recognition value of the title when the movie version appears?

Weighing all these factors, as well as others germane to each specific book, the editor decides whether to bid for the book and, if so, how much.

A lot has been written about bidding for paperback rights. Little of it is conclusive, including the mathematics. It is inconclusive because just about every "big" or potentially "big" book has its own particulars of time and place. With less-than-big books, the bidding parameters are a bit more established, but surprises are possible. The parameters for books that will be paperback originals or formula books such as Gothics and mysteries are also well-established, but guidelines are not firm in this area either. So much depends on how everyone involved "feels" about a particular deal.

A potentially "big" or almost-big book may be put out for paperback bids either before or sometime after hardcover publication: before, if the hardcover publisher is not entirely sure that the book will be a winner and is willing to settle for half-a-loaf; after, if the hardcover firm is reasonably sure that the book's hardcover success will drive up the price for the paperback rights.

Whichever the timing, the hardcover publisher or the author's literary agent or both of them let it be known that by a certain date, bids will be entertained from paperback houses for reprint rights to a book which, for purposes of this discussion, we will title *The Dopey Club*. Those inviting the bidding may set a number of conditions: There may be a "floor" price, beneath which no bids will be considered; there may be only one round of bids or there may be any number of rounds of bids; or one paperback house, perhaps because it published the author's earlier work in paperback or perhaps because it is corporately related to the hardcover house, may have the right to make a final bid, topping all the others.

The paperback editor, at a firm we will call Blockbuster Books, considers a number of factors and may consult with his firm's financial officers. *The Dopey Club*, published two months previously in hardcover, is a novel containing a nicely-balanced mixture of sex, narcotics and thinly disguised show biz personalities. Far from a triumph of literary style, it got mixed reviews of the sort that nevertheless could be described as "good sell." It had a respectable hardcover first printing of 15,000 copies, backed by a respectable advertising budget of $15,000. Before the book's publication, two chapters appeared in a big-circulation men's magazine. A small book club specializing in male-oriented subjects made the book a dual selection. The book has not yet hit any best seller lists but might make it to the bottom rungs because the very photo-genic author, Lucinda Lautrec, is currently on a tour of local TV talk shows. Lucinda's three previous books did not make the best seller lists either, but two of them did pretty well in paperback—reportedly about 150,000 and 250,000 copies, respectively—for another house.

Studying all these factors and considering how well his firm has done in the past with books like *The Dopey Club,* the editor makes some first, tentative decisions. Just as the agent and hardcover publisher set a basement figure, the editor in his own mind sets a ceiling figure, above which Blockbuster Books will not bid. He decides that *The Dopey Club* is worth no more to his firm than a bid of $250,000. He will open with a bid of $150,000. The basement figure specified is $100,000; by bidding $50,000 above that figure, the editor hopes to scare off some of the competition. He will then go by stages to his top figure of $250,000.

Essentially, a bid is a guarantee against the royalties which the paperback will earn. On royalties actually earned, Blockbuster Books is proposing to pay Lucinda 8 percent of retail price on the first 150,000 copies sold, 10 percent for the next 200,000 and 12½ percent on sales thereafter. At a retail price of $1.75 (not unusual for this kind of book), *The Dopey Club* would have to sell over 1 million copies in order to earn back a $250,000 advance. Drawing on past experience, the editor thinks the book will sell that well.

That, or something like it, would be the reasoning in a sane business. But paperback rights auctions are rarely sane. Firms have been known to bid outrageous sums—$1 million is no longer unthinkable—which they know will not be earned back for years, if ever, because they are trying to establish a reputation in the trade for doing "big" books. The $1 million book, then, may become a kind of loss leader, carrying the rest of the publisher's line with it into outlets where the line has been underrepresented. In the face of that kind of competition, some paperback firms stay out of big-money auctions altogether. Their lists may be relatively lackluster as a result, but their financial statements may be healthier.

To continue the story of *The Dopey Club:* In the second round of bidding, the auction quickly rises to Blockbuster's preset ceiling of $250,000; Blockbuster's bid of $250,000 has been matched by one other. The editor then asks himself: "If I was willing to go to $250,000, why not $275,000?" "OK," he tells himself, and for safety adds another $5,000. His $280,000 carries the day. The firm that had topping privileges, because it published Lucinda's earlier books, dropped out at the last minute. ("What do they know," the Blockbuster editor may ask himself, "that I don't know?" But he may reassure himself with the news that there have been rumors of movie interest in *The Dopey Club*. The reassurance is no more tangible than that, but the editor is glad to have it.)

Blockbuster Books now has *The Dopey Club*. Lucinda has her $280,000, which she must share with her hardcover publisher. For many years, a 50-50 split of paperback rights income was common, and it is still common enough to apply to Lucinda (who must also pay her agent 10 percent of her share). Some best-selling authors have succeeded in getting the split tilted in their favor to 60-40 or 70-30, and a few have been able to keep 100 percent of their paperback rights money. Typically, this has been accomplished by making the paperback publisher the originating publisher, with hardcover rights then assigned to a hardcover house—either an independent or one with the same corporate ownership as the paperback house. Such prepaperback hardcover preparation has brought major commercial success, through specially tailored advertising and publicity and nonpaperback subsidiary rights sales of the hardcover, to quite a number of books and authors in the marketplace where their prime sale was predestined: the paperback market. A case in point is author Harold Robbins, whose insistence on getting 100 percent of his paperback royalties was a prime reason for his paperback publisher, Pocket Books, to establish its separate Trident Press hardcover division.

Blockbuster Books must sell about 1.3 million copies of *The Dopey Club* in order to justify its $280,000 expenditure. Few people in the firm are likely to think about the book that way.

Books tend to be regarded as individual profit-and-loss statements only when they are very successful, an occasion for self-congratulation by all concerned on their wise, far-sighted investment in the book. On books that are something less than big successes, a book's modest profit or modest (or big) loss tends to be viewed against the pluses and minuses of the whole list during the month or quarter or year under consideration. In planning the publication of a book in paperback, the price paid for it is likely to have only a subliminal impact upon those involved.

Under terms of the agreement, Blockbuster cannot publish *The Dopey Club* until nine months after the publication of the hardcover edition or three months after the book's last appearance on a national hardcover best seller list, whichever comes later. These or similar restrictions on paperback publication are becoming increasingly common, and they seem to have no inhibiting effect on the prices paid in rights auctions. On the contrary, long life on a hardcover best seller list is generally regarded as an augury of additional success for the paperback.

Taking the time restrictions into consideration Blockbuster sets a tentative publication month for *The Dopey Club*. The tentativeness of the date is in part a function of the other books that Blockbuster has tentatively scheduled for that month. Many publishers fill each month's "package" of titles by categories: five or six novels, a Western, a mystery, four or five nonfiction titles, a few school titles and one hoped-for paperback best seller. Under such a system, it is thought bad to have too many new or reissued mysteries, for example, out in the marketplace competing with each other in the same month. Some publishers do not so categorize each month's list. Most publishers set a numerical limit on the titles they will publish each month, but some regularly and consciously exceed their own preset limits.

For *The Dopey Club*, the various departments within Blockbuster start planning soon after the reprint rights have been acquired. A lot of planning has to be done, for very little is spontaneous about the publication of a book that has been the subject of a spirited rights auction. Salesmen, executives in publicity, promotion and advertising, maybe someone in management, all read the book, or at least some of it. (The editor, presumably but not necessarily, has already read it.) Month of publication is confirmed, though it may be changed later. The month selected, it turns out, is a rather lean one for Blockbuster, and *The Dopey Club* becomes, rather *faute de mieux,* that month's hoped-for best seller. As such, it will get the full marketing treatment. Those movie rumors are getting stronger, and everyone uses that to justify a big sales pitch.

Nine months before the month of publication, Blockbuster holds a preprint meeting on all of the titles it will publish nine months hence. Attended by representatives of management and of the sales, editorial, publicity, promotion and advertising departments, this meeting has as its prime objective the setting of the size of first printings of nine-months-from-now's books. In this, the key people are the sales managers for Blockbuster Books' principal marketing areas: IDs, chain stores, jobbers, trade bookstores, Canada and export.

In this task of setting, however tentatively, the size of initial printings, publishers tend to think in terms of "track records" and of tightly defined categories: How well did this author's last book do for us? If the firm has never published the author before (and Blockbuster has never published Lucinda Lautrec before), how well did we do with our last show-biz-sex-narcotics-sleeping-around-sort of homosexual book?

In reaching such a judgment, the sales managers have available to them computerized information on past performances of earlier Blockbuster titles in the various markets. But at this time with *The Dopey Club,* euphoria is running a bit high: these movie interests really seem to be materializing, and Lucinda herself has agreed to go on yet another local TV-radio "talk" tour (indeed, you couldn't have kept her away from any available microphone or camera with an axe). And so, the sales managers pencil in quantities for their respective markets: 600,000 copies for IDs, 10,000 for chains, 15,000 for jobbers, 25,000 for trade bookstores serviced directly, 6,000 for Canada, 6,000 for export. That's a total of 662,000 copies—far too short of the theoretical break-even point, but no one is thinking much about that. A disproportionately large share goes through ID channels.

Six months before publication, a similar meeting is held. But this time, tentative cover art is available for inspection and comment. The importance of cover art cannot be overemphasized. The picture on the cover may be a book's only advertisement to the reading public. Or, in the case of a putative best seller, cover art may provide the keynote of the whole promotional campaign behind the book. The book's hardcover jacket may have been so successful as a merchandising symbol that it will be incorporated almost literally for the paperback edition. Or the hardcover jacket may be deemed unsuitable for the mass market, and a totally new cover concept will be commissioned.

Established cover artists comand handsome fees, as limitless in their way as are advances for authors, and it is not unusual for such an artist to be on a long-term exclusive contract with a specific publisher.

A whole body of expertise has grown up about what kinds of cover art sell books. (Snakes, guns or glasses of booze, for instance, are "out" in the mass market; female anatomy is "in," probably forever.) Experts in this area talk almost exclusively about their successes—how such-and-such a cover, no matter how accidentally arrived at, made a book literally "jump off the racks." Almost never do they talk about the covers of books that did not sell well.

At this cover meeting, print orders tentatively set three months earlier may be revised on the basis of late-breaking developments. Cover prices are set, if they were not set earlier, or revised if the group deems that necessary. Because of mass market paperback publishers' tightly categorized thinking, decision making at this prepublication stage is fairly routine. A meeting of an hour and a half or two hours can take care of a month's proposed production of, say, 30 titles. Nevertheless, these decisions involve a lot of money, for the company will be printing perhaps 5 million copies of the 30 titles.

While cognizant of computerized reports of past performances, publishers' sales managers may inflate indicated quantities by as much as 25 percent, particularly in the ID area, knowing that accounts will cut their suggested allotments no matter what their amount is. Publishers say that they no longer force-feed IDs or other accounts, but the "suggestion" of quantities can be pretty heavy. Blockbuster Books' salesmen will be calling on IDs to push *The Dopey Club* four months before publication. The salesmen's success or failure in reaching the suggested quantities for each ID are of vital importance. As they report back to the home office with their sales figures, final adjustments are made in the print order. Blockbuster's direct accounts—big bookstores, drug and variety chains, etc.—are visited by salesmen two months in advance of publication. By that time, the presses are beginning to roll.

The advertising, promotion and publicity departments are rolling, too. Up through the 1950s, paperback publishers pretty much limited their advertising and promotion efforts to in-store materials like posters and rack cards. Recognizing that consumer demand must be created as well as serviced, paperback publishers have gone substantially into space advertising, especially off-the-book pages, have become increasingly courageous about radio and TV advertising and have experimented with more offbeat (offbeat for books, that is) media such as bus and subway posters. Since *The Dopey*

Club is going to get "big book" treatment, it will be both advertised in suitable publications and featured with special floor and counter display fixtures and window streamers for dealers.

Paperbacks are not reviewed as widely as hardcover books, probably because review space is at a premium and the majority of paperbacks are reprints. But some magazines and newspapers do review paperbacks, at least periodically. In the hope that they will do so with *The Dopey Club,* the publicity department sends them press releases about the book and the author and review copies of the book. The publicity department schedules Lucinda's imminent assault on local broadcasters, and it notifies local stores as to when the author will be in their cities.

Those, in summary, are the standard prepublication moves. In addition, a specific book may suggest custom-tailored marketing strategy. Once published, a book is basically on its own. Will it "show legs" and "jump off the shelves?" Will it die, quickly and quietly, to be replaced by one of next month's releases? Or will its performance lie somewhere in between? If it is anything less than an instant success, it is not likely to get any more promotion, though there have been exceptions: books which started slowly but which, under the publisher's tender, loving care, built up respectable heads of steam.

The Dopey Club turned out to be a middling performer in the market. Had the planets been in a different phase, perhaps it could have been a tremendous hit, grossing hundreds of thousands of dollars for all concerned, or a tremendous flop, costing likewise hundreds of thousands. It went back to press once, for 50,000 copies. The movie interest never amounted to anything. Three months after publication, the book was effectively dead. A year after publication, with all the unsold returns counted, Blockbuster Books could figure that of the 712,000 copies it had printed, it had sold 354,000 and taken back 357,000. Another 1000 went for in-house use. Note that the returns greatly exceeded the size of the second printing; the disparity reflects the long time it can take before the publisher actually knows what is taking place in the market. By the time these sad figures were finally totaled, they represented little more than a footnote at Blockbuster Books, to be exhumed only when Lucinda or someone much like Lucinda came in with another book, their lesson to be heeded or, more likely, largely ignored. Mass market paperbacking is an industry populated by incurable optimists.

The birth of a trade paperback is less jazzy, and the life span may be considerably longer. The number of dollars and the number of copies are smaller. Distribution is primarily to bookstores and book jobbers. Marketing can be targeted to college art historians, to mechanical engineers or to whatever audience is deemed appropriate for the book. But because of the book's relatively low cover price, the use of direct mail is rarely justified for a single paperback or even for a related group of them. The jackpot markets for trade paperbacks are through bookstores and as college textbooks. Colleges remain the spiritual home of trade paperbacks.

An advance to an author for a trade paperback will usually be a few thousand dollars. It might be one thousand or less. Sometimes, in cases where a publisher issues his own hardcover title as a trade paperback, there might be no additional advance. The royalty scale will be between 5 percent and 8 percent of list price. The first printing will be between 4000 and 10,000 copies. With trade paperbacks published by mass market firms and merchandised through mass market channels, these figures will be considerably higher.

The trade paperback will have a longer time in the market to prove its salability than its mass market counterpart. It takes a long time to secure those course adoptions and build a word-of-mouth reputation for a book. Most of the prepublication steps that go to mass market paperbacks are also applied to trade paperbacks. But with trade paperbacks, the pace is less frantic (although as mass market publishers have branched into trade paperbacks, they have stepped up the pace).

For just about any publisher, whether hardcover or paperback, mass market or trade, the sublime objective is to create a book that will become a backlist staple, selling year after year and requiring little additional expenditure for promotion. This goal has characterized trade paperback publishing from its modern beginnings in the 1950s; indeed, the first of the modern trade paperbacks were reprints of books already well established in the academic community. Backlist considerations have characterized a substantial segment of mass market paperback publishing, too; the school-suitable titles, the reprints of old and modern classics, Dr. Spock's book on child care are all backlist. For teachers especially, it is a great feather in the academic cap to be the author of a long-lived paperback, for of all the various kinds of books, paperbacks are most fashionable on campus. Those mass market publishers which have added a trade paperback publishing capacity have also added a publishing approach that can give longer life to books that are not obvious backlist candidates but require time in the market to find their audience.

A common factor among mass market firms that went under is that they had little or no backlist. The strong publishers do have backlist, and they are paying more attention to it, particularly in specialized markets such as schools and religious institutions.

Chapter 9

Quick History of an "Extra"

"Extras," by whatever name (different firms use different names; "instant books" is perhaps the generic), demonstrate mass market paperback publishing operating at its full potential. "Extras" are books on subjects of surpassing national or international concern, extremely timely and therefore extremely perishable. The faster they get to market, the more copies they will sell. It is a newspaper editorial concept applied to book publishing. Hence, extras.

Bantam published the first extra in 1964, *Report of the Warren Commission on the Assassination of President Kennedy*. It sold 1.5 million copies and added a whole new dimension to paperback publishing.

Since then, "extras" have included a Pope's visit to the U.S., the Apollo 11 moon flight, the 1967 Arab-Israeli war, the 1968 Detroit race riots, the New York City power blackout and the *Kerner Commission Report on Civil Disorders*.

Following is a chronology* of an "extra"—the edited Watergate tapes that Bantam published under the title, *The White House Transcripts.*

April 29, 1974. President Nixon tells the nation that he is releasing the edited tape transcripts.

April 30. The transcripts, a 1308-page document, are issued by the Government Printing Office.

May 2. Bantam announces that it will publish the transcripts as a paperback, in collaboration with the *New York Times.* (Dell, on the same day, announces that it, too, will publish a paperback edition, with the *Washington Post* as collaborator.)

That afternoon, 1300 pages of copy for Bantam's edition arrive at the W.F. Hall Printing Company's Diversey Avenue plant in Chicago. Hall has already scheduled overtime shifts. Bantam has notified Hall, which prints most of Bantam's books, that paperbacks already in production can be set aside for the Watergate Tapes paperback.

By Delta Airlines jet, Hall sends the copy to the typesetter, the E.T. Lowe Publishing Company in Nashville. An hour after the copy arrives, it is being set by four tape-driven Teletype linecasters and five manual linotypes.

May 4. At 4 A.M., Lowe finishes setting the transcripts' more than 250,000 words. All the type proofs have been read twice by a team of seven proofreaders. The typesetters pause to await arrival of the book's introduction by R.W. Apple of the *New York Times,* and other editorial material from New York.

At 9 A.M., Ray Little, Bantam's vice-president for production, arrives in Nashville.

At 6 P.M., Bantam editors Judy Knipe and Jean Highland arrive in Nashville with the remaining copy. In Chicago, mechanicals for the cover arrive at Regensteiner Press.

*Condensed from an article in *Inland Printer/American Lithographer,* June 1974.

May 5. By early morning, typesetting is completed. Lowe starts making up page forms. Bantam editors supervise last-minute changes and OK page proofs. Lowe begins making the first of 148 six-page bakelite molds.

In Chicago, Regensteiner completes separations for the cover. Plates are made in the evening.

May 6. The first group of molds is finished, but there will be no commercial jet to Chicago until tomorrow. A private jet is chartered and takes off from Nashville at 8 P.M. with the first molds. The jet makes a round trip, returning to Nashville to pick up Little, the two editors and the rest of the molds.

May 7. The jet lands in Chicago shortly after midnight. The molds are rushed to Hall's Diversey plant, where last-minute typesetting and mold preparation are completed. In eight hours, four men and two machines turn out the book's rubber plates—an average of 110 plates an hour. Hall rushes the rubber plates to its Normandy Avenue plant. (This plant produces an average of 1.5 million paperbacks every 24 hours, five days a week.)

Between 1 A.M. and 4 A.M., Regensteiner prints the covers—32-up—on a four-color, 77-inch Miehle offset press. Covers are shipped to Hall, where they are varnished and cut apart.

The rubber molds are mounted on Mylar sheets, and the sheets are wrapped around the cylinders of most of Hall's two-unit Strachan & Henshaw flexographic presses. Each press prints two-up 32-page signatures, or 128 separate pages. The plates go on the presses at 8 A.M. The first books come off the Sheridan patent-binding lines at 6 P.M. Elapsed production time: 91 hours.

As a result of orders received from IDs and Bantam's own salesmen, the original print order of 225,000 has been doubled and doubled again, finally reaching 1.4 million copies. This will require 700 tons of specialty newsprint. Bantam digs into the two-month inventory of 27 pound newsprint it keeps at Hall, primarily to reprint backlist books. It will return the inventory to its normal level later.

As the finished books come off Hall's bindery lines, they are packed in 10-book and 25-book cartons. The first shipment of 5000 copies goes by truck to O'Hare airport and is loaded on a plane to Washington.

By the end of the day, 100,000 copies have been bound and shipped.

May 8. At 7:30 A.M., 5000 copies arrive at the District News Company in Washington. At 8 A.M., the first copies are on sale at a bookstore on Pennsylvania Avenue one block from the White House.

Chapter 10
Boom and Bust and Boom and . . .

When Pocket Books started the modern mass market paperback "revolution" in 1939, paperback books already had a long tradition and a high mortality rate in the history of American publishing. In Colonial times, sermons, government reports and almanacs were printed as paperbacks. Between 1777 and 1782, some 190 volumes were published in John Bell's British Poets series. They were paperbacks and sold for eight shillings, a bargain price. In 1831, the Boston Society for the Diffusion of Knowledge began publishing the paperback American Library of Vital Knowledge. These were self-help books with an irreproachably high moral tone. That high moral tone probably was largely responsible for the demise of the series.

In the 1830s and 1840s, many newspapers began inserting unbound books in the papers in order to avoid the higher postal rate on books. Cut-throat price competition ensued as more and more newspapers entered this field. The Post Office Department ended this particular paperback revolution when, in 1843, it slapped the higher book rate on newspapers carrying the book inserts.

Dime novels, which were stories with frontier themes, had a bright but short-lived success during the Civil War and the years immediately afterward. When the price of paper declined sharply in the 1870s, newspapers for a time reentered the paperback book field and issued novels and "specials" at 10 or 20 cents each as circulation builders.

The big paperback development of the last quarter of the 19th century were the so-called Cheap Libraries. These were mostly reprints of British and French novels, and they were cheap because they were pirated: the authors received no royalties. Anyone could publish these books in the United States, and for a time it seemed that just about everyone did. There was great duplication of titles and great price competition. Shabby to begin with, the books in the Cheap Libraries became even shabbier as production costs were cut to meet intensified price competition. By 1885, there were 5000 of these paperbacks in print, and another 1500 titles were being added every year. The Cheap Library development probably would have choked to death on its own market glut. Before that could take place, the Cheap Library business abruptly ended in 1891 when the U.S. signed an international copyright agreement that effectively stopped the nation's long, dubious position as a literary pirate. But as late as 1905, *Price's Catalog of Paper Books* listed thousands of titles priced at 10-25 cents, many of them in public domain or holdovers from before 1891. They were distributed mainly by news distributors to newspaper stores.

In the 1920s and 1930s, paperback programs cropped up in isolated ways. For example, a Girard, Kansas, eccentric named E. Haldemann-Julius published hundreds of five-cent paperback Little Blue Books which were sold almost entirely by mail. Most of these were self-help books designed to improve a reader's competence in sexual and other areas of life, but the Little Blue Books program also included more lasting fare. Among the latter was a series on philosophy by Will Durant, a young instructor at Columbia University. Simon & Schuster acquired copyright to the Durant pamphlets, the basis for Will and Ariel Durant's enormously successful hardcover *Story of Civilization* project, which started in 1935 and now numbers a dozen volumes. In the 1930s, Modern Age Books came along, publishing unabashedly highbrow titles, mostly originals, as 25-, 35- and 50-cent paperbacks. Highbrow plus low price equalled no success, and Modern Age switched to hardcover in 1939.

The paperback tradition in Europe was more literary than the tradition in the U.S. For a serious reader, the European paperback was a bargain, as American tourists discovered. They brought home the various French publishers' paperbacks and, notably, the Tauchnitz Editions and the Albatross Books from Germany. Why, many of these tourists asked, were American books so much more expensive? As they might have learned, the difference was not between paper and cloth binding, for the American and the European book had to go through the same processes of printing, collating, folding and stitching. The difference had more to do with the European and American differences of money value, labor costs, and economies of uniform format and the rate of royalties paid to authors.

American Pocket Books' immediate ancestor was Penguin Books, the paperback program that Allen Lane started in England in 1935. Lane's primary concern was editorial, not marketing. He wanted to publish quality reprints, at a sixpenny price, and sell them through regular book channels. As he visited major booksellers with the list of his first ten proposed titles, Lane was told that the titles were fine, but that the proposed format was eccentric and the sixpenny price would not give booksellers a sufficient operating profit. Lane then approached a segment of the mass market and called on buyers for some variety chain stores. There, he was told that price and format were fine but that the titles might be too intellectual. According to legend, the wife of a Woolworth buyer told her husband that she would eagerly buy such books if they existed, and Woolworth placed an order. Once the books were published, Woolworth, after a day or two, placed a reorder. Penguins, their editorial quality intact, had cracked a corner of the mass market and were well launched.

In America, Robert Fair de Graff had watched the Penguin developments in England with interest. De Graff had a thorough training in hardcover reprint publishing, first with Doubleday and later as operator and part owner of Blue Ribbon Books. He was pleased that Penguins had proved themselves in chain stores, for he proposed to take paperbacks even further into the mass market: to drug stores and newsstands via the channels which magazine publishers had developed.

Reprint publishing in America at that time was hardcover, and the firm of Grosset & Dunlap dominated the field. When de Graff told Grosset executives that he proposed to do *paperback* reprints, the people at Grosset raised no objections. Perhaps they were recalling the fact that the paperback publishing road in America was littered with dead bodies.

De Graff had a publishing blueprint that he thought would work and set out in search of partners. He found them at Simon & Schuster. M. Lincoln Schuster, after he had listened to de Graff's plans, told de Graff that he had been playing around with a similar idea himself: a Twentieth Century Library of paperbacks to retail for 20 cents apiece.

Schuster suggested a 25-cent cover price. De Graff suggested the name "Pocket Books." Whether the name choice was casual or profound, competitors to come would hate it for years. Because for years, all paperbacks, regardless of their imprints, were regarded by readers as "pocket books," and the name was a protected trademark.

For reprint rights, de Graff was offering hardcover publishers a royalty of 4 percent of his proposed 25-cent cover price and an advance of $500, both to be split 50-50 between author and original publisher. Most publishers grabbed the offer, perhaps in the belief that de Graff's scheme would never work and that the $500 would be found money.

Pocket Books' original capital was $30,000, 51 percent put up by de Graff and 49 percent by Simon & Schuster. De Graff and a secretary moved into a two-room office at Simon & Schuster. The single telephone was listed to "Pocket Books," and a number of leather salesmen made hopeful calls . . . and went away muttering darkly.

De Graff printed 2000 test copies of a Pocket Book edition of Pearl Buck's "The Good Earth" and showed them around to potential retail and wholesale buyers. Space ads and a 50,000-piece direct mail campaign invited readers to order books from a 52-title list (some of these titles were actually under reprint contracts at Pocket Books, but most were not) and send in money at 25 cents a book. Respondents were asked to indicate, on a prepared checklist, whether they ever bought books, where they bought them, what kinds they bought and what kinds they wanted to buy. Those who sent money for titles that did not yet exist as Pocket Books were put off with form letters stating that the program was still experimental.

De Graff's prime orientation was to marketing rather than editorial. But he and his Simon & Schuster colleagues had sound instincts about the kind of editorial quality that results in sales. The first ten Pocket Book titles were selected, and first printings of 10,000 each were authorized.* New York City was to be the first test market. The biggest initial orders were from Macy's and Liggett's. De Graff had originally planned to sell

*The first ten: *Lost Horizon* by James Hilton, *Wake Up and Live* by Dorothea Brande, *Five Great Tragedies* by William Shakespeare, *Topper* by Thorne Smith, *The Murder of Roger Ackroyd* by Agatha Christie, *Enough Rope* by Dorothy Parker, *Wuthering Heights* by Emily Bronte, *The Way of All Flesh* by Samuel Butler, *The Bridge of San Luis Rey* by Thornton Wilder, and *Bambi* by Felix Salten. *The Good Earth,* which had been Pocket Books' trial balloon, became Pocket Books' eleventh title.

his books only outside traditional book trade channels, but Cedric Crowell of the Doubleday bookstore chain, at that time president of the American Booksellers Association, persuaded him to include bookstores in his paperback revolution.

The New York test was a complete success. On publication date, Pocket Books' single telephone was jammed with reorders from existing customers and orders from stores that had just heard about the Pocket Books phenomenon and wanted a part in it. As part of his blueprint for mass distribution, de Graff had resources of paper and high-speed press time available, and the presses rolled. Distribution essentially went three simultaneous routes: direct to stores, to the American News Company, and to the independent magazine wholesalers. Hardcover publishers, noting Pocket Books' initial triumph, got on the bandwagon and cooperated in signing reprint licenses.

Soon after the start of World War II, paper rationing was imposed. But Leon Shimkin, the Simon & Schuster partner primarily in charge of business management, was able to make arrangements with several publishers who were underutilizing their paper quotas. With the war on in earnest, Pocket Books was able to sell anything it could print to the well-heeled civilian population in search of recreation, to the military and to the Red Cross. Approximately 25 million Pocket Books were shipped overseas by various wartime agencies.

In the book publishing industry, the wartime boom led to paterns of thinking which, though perhaps it was unnoticed at the time, would pose postwar problems. For during the war, there were, almost literally, no returns of unsold books. And in mass market publishing, returns are an unavoidable fact of life. As it happened, it was fortunate that Pocket Books, together with Simon & Schuster, was acquired in 1944 by Marshall Field, the Chicago millionaire and liberal newspaper publisher. Field's capital helped Pocket Books survive the postwar flood of returns that almost swamped this latest paperback "revolution."

Pocket Books soon had competitors, though when it started, these competitors were struggling infants compared to de Graff's well-organized, well-financed operation. Out of the magazine field came Avon Books in 1940, Popular Library in 1942 and Dell Books in 1943. Another potential competitor— though actually quite a different kind of operation—was on the scene the same month as Pocket (July 1939), when Penguin Books opened an American branch office.

Ian Ballantine, head of Penguin's American office, was an American graduate of the London School of Economics who had written his thesis on the economics of paperback publishing. Ballantine owned 49 percent of the American company, and Allen Lane owned 51 percent. The original function of the American company was to import Penguins from England and, through salesmen working on commission, sell them to bookstores. When the war cut off supplies from England, Ballantine became not an importer but a publisher. To qualify for a paper quota, he published war books, both those he originated and those published in a joint imprint arrangement with *Infantry Journal.* In the American style, he published books with pictures on the covers, not the austere type-only style of Penguin covers.

When the war in Europe ended in 1945, Allen Lane visited his American outpost. He liked nothing he saw, especially the covers. His and Ballantine's differences were irreconcilable, and Ballantine left. At Penguin, Ballantine was succeeded by Kurt Enoch, a German immigrant publisher who had been a founder of Albatross Books, and Victor Weybright, who during the war was on the U.S. Ambassador's staff at the Court of St. James. Ballantine took two associates with him, editor Walter Pitkin, Jr., and treasurer Sidney Kramer. To keep a paper allocation, he also took the arrangement with *Infantry Journal.* And he hired the Curtis Circulation Company to act as his distributor to magazine channels.

Ballantine still needed financial backing, and he went to Grosset & Dunlap, the hardcover reprint firm that six years

71

previously had essentially given de Graff a green light for Pocket Books. Grosset, a long-established (1898) company, since 1944 had been owned jointly by Book-of-the-Month Club, Harper & Brothers, Little, Brown & Company, Random House and Charles Scribner's Sons. Together the five had acquired Grosset in the face of a perceived threat that Marshall Field was about to buy it. They felt that with Simon & Schuster, Pocket Books and Grosset under one corporate umbrella, the Field group of book publishers would be too powerful.

Having acquired Grosset, the five publisher-owners were still uncompetitive with Field's paperback operation at Pocket Books when Ballantine arrived in search of capital. What Ballantine had to recommend him, in addition to his track record at Penguin, was his close association with Curtis. Without a major national distributor, a paperback line would be difficult to start, and Curtis was a giant in the field. And so, Grosset organized a paperback subsidiary in August 1945. It was called Bantam Books. Its colophon, a rooster, set out to do battle with Pocket Books' colophon, a kangaroo.

Bantam published its first 20 books on January 3, 1946.* They were priced at 25 cents each, and they had first printings of about 200,000 copies each. Bantam then settled down to a production rate of about four titles per month. Since the books were distributed like magazines and since Curtis was the distributor, it was natural that the editorial mix should be like that of the *Saturday Evening Post:* lots of mysteries and

---

*Bantam's first 20: *Life on the Mississippi* by Mark Twain, *The Gift Horse* by Frank Gruber, *Nevada* by Zane Grey, *Evidence of Things Seen* by Elizabeth Daly, *Scaramouche* by Rafael Sabatini, *A Murder by Marriage* by Robert G. Deal, *The Grapes of Wrath* by John Steinbeck, *The Great Gatsby* by F. Scott Fitzgerald, *Rogue Male* by Geoffrey Household, *South Moon Under* by Marjorie Kinnan Rawlings, *Wind, Sand and Stars* by Antoine de Saint-Exupery, *The Last Time I Saw Paris* by Eliot Paul, *Then There Were Three* by Geoffrey Homes, *The Town Cried Murder* by Leslie Ford, *Mr. and Mrs. Cugat* by Isabel Scott Rorick, *Meet Me in St. Louis* by Sally Benson, *Seventeen* by Booth Tarkington, *What Makes Sammy Run* by Budd Schulberg, *One More Spring* by Robert Nathan, *Oil for the Lamps of China* by Alice Tisdale Hobart.

Westerns, a few solid novels, not much culture. To compete on newsstands with magazines, the covers on the books were somewhat sexy; the cover on an edition of *Little Women,* for instance, showed some cleavage.

The paperback field drew more new entries. In 1948, Victor Weybright and Kurt Enoch, like Ballantine before them, had a falling out with Allen Lane and left American Penguin to form New American Library. NAL's early Signet and Mentor books were in the same format as Penguins, somewhat larger than the early Pockets and Bantams. They were distributed by Fawcett, a magazine publisher which then had no paperback line. Barred by a no-compete clause in its contract with NAL, Fawcett could not publish reprints. But it started a line of Gold Medal original paperbacks, and when its agreement with NAL terminated, it added Crest and Premier reprint lines.

Avon, Dell and Popular Library were publishing more paperbacks. More magazine publishers came into the field: Almat Publishing with Pyramid Books, A.A. Wyn with Ace Books, Berkley Publishing with Berkley Books.

Entering the 1950s, it appeared that American paperback publishing would again self-destruct. The market was glutted. Quantities of unsold books were the barometers of the problem. Profits were dropping, and production costs were rising. Publishers began raising cover prices: to 35 cents, to 50 cents. Industry confidence was shaken when a Congressional committee attacked allegedly smutty covers. It was shaken further when Senator Joseph McCarthy charged that U.S. Information Agency libraries overseas were full of subversive books. One report, in June 1953, said that 175 million unsold paperbacks were piled up in warehouses around the country. Pocket Books dumped several million books into an abandoned canal lock near Buffalo.

With independent wholesalers, most publishers at that time operated on an "exchange" basis: the ID kept unsold books until the publisher said they could be returned for an equivalent value in new books. In the mid-1950s, one publisher after another shifted to a magazine system whereby the IDs needed only to return covers for credit, shredding the body of the books. This has eliminated a lot of freight charges for unsalable books, but returns remain the industry's largest single problem.

The industry weathered the returns crisis of the 1950s, which was aggravated by the American News Company's withdrawal from book and magazine distribution. Some publishers went under. Those remaining ate a lot of unsold books.

There were corporate and personnel changes. Ballantine left Bantam in 1952, and for a year and a half Bantam operated without a president. Then Oscar Dystel, who had a strong background in magazine publishing but none in books, was brought in. In 15 years, his leadership would bring Bantam to its present position as the world's undisputed Number One in paperbacks.

Ballantine started his own independent paperback firm, Ballantine Books, and began by publishing paperback originals simultaneously with hardcovers issued by other firms.(This technique had been tried by others, notably Simon & Schuster which in the late 1940s issued simultaneous hardcover and paperback editions of some titles, thus urging these books on to hoped-for best sellerdom. The tactic had mixed results.)

Marshall Field died in 1957, and Pocket Books reacquired its corporate self (as, separately, did Simon & Schuster). De Graff had retired some years earlier to pursue other, private interests. In 1961, Pocket Books became a public company, putting 20 percent of its shares on the market.

Mergers, conglomerates and stock offerings dominated book publishing industry news from the late 1950s to the mid-1970s, and paperback publishing was not unaffected. In 1959,

Hearst bought Avon, and the Avon imprint began a sporadic resurgence that culminated under the leadership of Peter Mayer,one of the industry's brightest "young Turks," who became publisher at Avon in 1968.

The Los Angeles Times-Mirror conglomerate bought NAL in 1960. Ballantine Books was sold to Intext, a publishing-correspondence school group, in 1968, and was sold again to Random House in 1973. Ian Ballantine and his wife, Betty, returned to Bantam Books to co-publish books under their own imprint, Peacock Press.

CBS bought Popular Library in 1971. Two hardcover firms acquired mass market capacity by buying ongoing firms: G.P. Putnam's purchased Berkley Books, and Harcourt Brace Jovanovich bought Pyramid Books. In October 1975, the Harcourt and Pyramid editorial departments were totally merged. William Jovanovich, chairman of the company, explained: "The hardcover business has changed dramatically, and this is our way of responding to that change. . . . We are losing money on too many hardcover books. . . . Our object is not to be self-enclosed. The object is to recognize the fact that paperback publishing is the perdurable force in our industry." All options—hardcover publishing or simultaneous trade paperback or mass market paperback "should be an organic part of one publishing department," Jovanovich said.

Pocket Books (and Simon & Schuster) was acquired in 1975 by Gulf & Western Industries, a multi-faceted conglomerate whose best known property is Paramount Pictures. Paperback Library, a small firm of no particular editorial distinction, was acquired by the Warner Communications conglomerate, which appears determined to use its ample resources to push Warner Paperback to a position of prominence in the paper-back field; for example, the company put a $2.5 million down payment on President Nixon's memoirs, sight unseen.

Bantam Books is an extraordinary case of How to Succeed in Publishing Despite Conglomerate Ownership. First owned by five hardcover houses, Bantam, in 1968, was bought by the National General Corporation, a firm primarily concerned with motion pictures. And in 1974, Bantam was acquired for $70 million by the Istituto Finanziario Industriale (IFI), a Turin-based conglomerate whose interests include Fiat automobiles, Cinzano vermouth, and Fratelli Fabbri, a Milan publishing and printing giant known for mediocre products, constant losses, and a checkered history (ironically, Gulf & Western holds a minority position in its equity). Bantam's success story is a reassuring one, for it is consistently characterized by top-quality books rising to the top of the market. Changes of ownership have not changed that, and there seems no reason to expect that the new Italian ownership will change that either.

Of the "Big Five" in mass market publishing, three are conglomerate owned (Bantam, Pocket Books and NAL), and two are independents (Fawcett and Dell). If one expands the group to a "Big Seven," to reflect Avon's brashness and Warner's well-funded aspirations, one adds two more conglomerates to the group. At this writing (August 1975), there is much speculation in publishing circles about the two remaining independents. Each is closely held, and the principal owners of each are of an age when people start to worry about things like estate taxes.

Chapter
11
Trade Paperbacks:
To Academe and Beyond

Doubleday's publication of the first six Anchor Books in 1953 has generally been accepted as the start of the modern trade paperback revolution. But this revolution, like the mass market one before it, had some immediate ancestors. They could be found in college bookstores. In no small way, the success of trade paperbacks has derived from a natural affinity that exists between college students and the paper bindings. The medium is at least a lot of the message.

In pre-Anchor days, college store paperback departments had a lot of mass market paperbacks, and now they have more than ever; these books are products of a system that places prime distribution reliance on magazine channels. What is distinctive about trade paperbacks, in addition to such matters as price and format, is that their distribution is primarily through book channels: bookstores and jobbers.

Among the first trade paperbacks in college stores were the excellent reprints and originals in science and technology issued by Dover Publications, a firm started in 1942. Dover has since broadened its editorial base, and science-technology now accounts for only about 10 percent of its output. Hayward Cirker, president of Dover, could be called the father of modern trade paperbacks, but he has never pressed the claim. Another early line came from Oceana Publications, specialist in books about the law. Some major hardcover reprint series, such as Modern Library, selectively paperbacked books which were being used in college classrooms. Some straight textbooks came out in paper bindings. The various college outline paperback series were long-time staples in college stores.

Academically oriented paperbacks were not really new, therefore, when the first Anchor Books appeared. What was new was that they were being published by a major firm, Doubleday, which had massive publicity and promotion resources that could make the first Anchors seem like a new phenomenon. In this, Doubleday was very successful. Jason Epstein, then a 23-year-old Doubleday editor, was given credit for conceiving the Anchor Books idea and was dubbed the father of trade paperbacks. Epstein himself later said the idea originated in the Doubleday manufacturing department. Doubleday is one of the few publishers that have their own book production machinery, and there is constant pressure at Doubleday to keep the presses rolling. One way to keep them rolling was to repackage older books of proven quality, both Doubleday books and those of other publishers, in paper covers to sell at attractive prices.

The first six Anchors carried prices of 85 cents to $1.25 and were unabashedly highbrow.* Highbrow paperback lines had failed in the past, but the large postwar college population made it unlikely that this time history would repeat itself.

That, at any rate, was the majority opinion among publishers, and the rush of firms to join this newest paperback revolution was giddy. Some of the new trade paperback lines

---

*The first six were *American Humor* by Constance Rourke, *Studies in Classic American Literature* by D.H. Lawrence, *The Idea of a Theater* by Francis Fergusson, *An Essay on Man* by Ernest Cassirer, *The Romance of Tristan and Iseult* by Joseph Bedier and *Charterhouse of Parma* by Stendhal.

were general; others were specialized in their editorial approaches. Hardly a field of literature, scholarship or human activity escaped the paperback fervor. Editors poured over backlists—theirs and others—like dedicated archaeologists. Books which had sat dormant in warehouses for years could suddenly command several thousand dollars in advances for reprint rights. Most university presses started their own paperback lists. Two major presses that at first stayed aloof, Harvard and Princeton, made right-of-first-refusal agreements with a trade firm, Atheneum, that was starting its own paperback line.

Some of the results of this gold rush approach were predictable. A number of new lines failed, either because they were unfocused editorially or underfinanced or both. For those that remained, title production soon outstripped the number of courses that might adopt the books and the shelf space available in stores that might display them. A national jobber which had been formed to distribute trade paperbacks, with warehouses in New York, the Midwest and California, failed because it expanded too rapidly on inadequate profit margins. Distribution has always been the Achilles Heel of American trade book publishing, and so it was with trade paperbacks.

Yet the idea behind trade paperbacks—quality books at sensible prices—is so sound that it survived the early shake-out period. Academic books published as original trade paperbacks were published simultaneously in hardcover, in the interest of attracting the library market, which historically was wary of fragile paper bindings. For example, Frederick A. Praeger, Inc., simultaneously published an average of 12,000 paperback and 5000 hardback copies of many of the books in its art, history and political science programs. A whole new book market developed somewhere between hardcover books and mass market paperbacks, with overlaps between. College stores, which previously had done little bookselling except for textbooks, developed respectable general book departments under the trade paperback impetus. Bookstores specializing in trade paperbacks blossomed in city neighborhoods which had never supported bookstores before.

Local jobbers came into being to wholesale trade paperbacks in their particular geographical areas. With success, they branched into other areas and also selectively added mass market paperbacks and hardcover books to their inventories. Some IDs selectively added trade paperbacks to their mass market book and magazine lines.

The National Association of College Stores gave the trade paperback industry a welcome measure of stability when it established a separate corporation, NACSCORP, to wholesale trade paperbacks to its bookstore members. Originally, NACSCORP was conceived as an adjunct to an NACS service which centrally processed student magazine subscriptions secured through its member stores, but the book business quickly outstripped the magazines. In 1974, NACS sold $2½ million worth of trade paperbacks, $550,000 worth of magazine subscriptions.

There is something in the trade paperback format not confined to a particular page size and not bound by hardcovers that inspires editorial creativity and experiment. Readers, in the same nebulous way, respond to this. For example, it is hard to imagine *The Whole Earth Catalog*—part book, part catalog, part lifestyle—as anything other than a trade paperback, and it was a most successful one. Some trade paperbacks are not, strictly speaking, books at all, like the bound collections of posters that have had very successful commercial careers. Many book buyers find gorgeous visuals, graphics and art reproductions even more gorgeous in paper covers; they would find the same materials in hardcovers too stuffy and forbidding. Mass market publishers were not unaware of this special ambiance when they expanded into trade paperbacks.

Trade Paperbacks: To Academe and Beyond

The same book can take a variety of forms to reach a variety of markets. A new market was there, and trade paperbacks, in a way that was not always certain, found it.

Chapter 12

The News of the Month in Review

In an average month, perhaps 1500, perhaps 2000 titles will be published in paperback. The total would include everything: mass market and trade books; popular, professional, religious, juvenile books; monographs and lowest common denominator kind of *kitsch*; reprints and originals; books making their first appearance in paperback and earlier paperbacks that have been repackaged or otherwise revivified.

They would all go into our hypothetical Paperback Parnassus bookstore.

In the same month, another 1500 or 2000 titles will go out of print and become unavailable, temporarily or permanently, in paperback. Their disappearance provides a degree of biological balance at Paperback Parnassus, though the net effect continues to be population explosion.

It is impossible to state title production figures with any assurance of statistical accuracy. The different monitoring agencies operate from different premises, but they do provide some guidelines.

The editors of *Paperbound Books in Print* reported that 11,000 new paperbacks were published in the first seven months of 1975. In the first five months of 1975, according to *PBIP,* 8000 titles went out of print. The new-title figure would not include some repackages and reissues.

Publishers Weekly and the Library of Congress, in a joint title-counting effort, found that 8700 trade paperbacks and 2802 mass market paperbacks were published in 1974. *Publishers Weekly* and the Library of Congress do not catalogue a lot of light fiction published in mass market paperback; to reflect that, their figure for mass books should be increased by perhaps 1500 titles. And they do not recatalogue books that have already appeared in paperback, although they might if a title has been unavailable for a significantly long period of time.

CPDA counted 4254 new paperbacks in 1974. It counts only books from mass market, ID-distributed lines, but it does count new packages.

A book reviewer looks at this flood of title production and must make a lot of initial decisions, mostly of a negative nature. As has already been noted, paperbacks are less widely reviewed than hardbacks, because the majority of paperbacks are reprints. Early in 1975, the *New York Times Book Review,* the most important general review medium, announced that it was expanding its paperback coverage. So far, the expansion has consisted of a weekly two-part (mass market and trade) paperback best seller list, a weekly chat feature about the paperback industry, plus periodic inclusions of paperbacks in round-up review columns devoted to genres such as mysteries.

Publishers Weekly devotes 2-4 pages a week to paperback reviews. Since this is a service for trade bookstore and jobber buyers, the reviews appear two or three months before the books are actually published. Space in the magazine is very limited, and the reviewer can cover only a fraction of 1 percent of a month's paperback titles. The selection of books for review seeks to evoke a wide popular spectrum. *Publishers Weekly* is saying, in effect: These are the books that may be expected to sell but that may be important for other reasons, too.

The selection provides some insight into the current editorial state of paperback publishing.

In a month, selected at random, during the spring of 1975, *Publishers Weekly* reviewed 78 paperbacks. About 55 percent were mass market paperbacks, 45 percent were trade. Forty-eight titles were originals: 18 nonfiction, 30 fiction. Of the 30 reprints, 22 were fiction, eight nonfiction.

Among the nonfiction originals were an exposé of an international financier, a collection of articles about financial scoundrels, a profile of a psychic, two psychiatric self-helps, three books about nutrition, self-help for single mothers, three travel books, a profile of a French filmmaker, a book about international conglomerates, a collection of Karl Marx essays, books about child rearing, China, show business and Egyptology. The subjects of the nonfiction reprints included the U.S. Supreme Court, astrophysics, Watergate, a mass murderer, the Bermuda Triangle, Sherlock Holmes, show business and nuclear physics.

Action themes predominated the fiction originals, followed by sex, Hollywood, the Old West (a movie tie-in), history, romance (not the same as sex), Dracula and Rod McKuen. Big-name authors among the fiction reprints were Susan Howitch, Philip Roth, Gore Vidal, Edward Gorey and Dorothy Eden, and other novels were about nuclear war, American politics, prize fights, romance, hospitals, families, prisons, department stores and the sea.

Perhaps a psychologist or a sociologist, studying this grab bag of paperbacks, could come up with some profound thoughts as to what it says about the quality of life—and hopes and fears—in America in mid-1975. Such an inquiry is beyond the scope of this volume and the competence of its author. Here we can say only that these books represent various editors' perceptions about life in America; and that they were picked for review because their perceptions seemed, for one reason or another, especially relevant. Some will reach very large audiences, the rest will find smaller ones.

The same can be said about the 99-plus percent of the month's books that were not selected for review. Some may be so emetic that they deserve no critical attention. Some may be so high- or narrow-brow that a general audience would never perceive them. All have their putative audiences.

The Paperback Parnassus bookstore would be impractical for more than economic reasons. Instead of having all those titles under one roof, it might be better to have them in a sequence of bazaar-like stalls, stretching to the horizon. A "specialist mass market" might seem a contradiction in terms, but it accurately describes the paperback market.

Chapter
13

Neurosis and the Crisis
of 1974-75

In 1974 and early 1975, mass market paperback publishing, after several years as book publishing's greatest growth sector, slowed like a quarter horse attempting six furlongs. In 1973, mass market publishers' receipts of $285.9 million (at retail, about $410 million) represented an increase of 13.1 percent over 1972 and 24.9 percent over 1971. But the 1974 total of $293.6 million (about $420 million at retail) was up a modest 2.7 percent over 1973—the worst growth record of any area of hardcover or paperback publishing. Paperback publishers' pretax net income was down from 6.2 percent in 1973 to 3.8 percent in 1974. And in the first months of 1975, mass market paperback sales were no better than even with 1974's performance. Worse yet, 1974's modest increase proved to be entirely caused by inflation; unit sales, 1973-74, were actually off by about 3.3 percent.

What had happened? It was tempting to blame the 1974-75 economic recession, but that failed as a probable cause for at least two reasons. First, no other category of books showed such a sharp slow-down. Second, paperbacks have always been considered recession-proof, for they are among the cheapest of all the entertainment and education media.

Was something wrong with the editorial product? It hardly seemed so. The mix of best sellers and category books was as it had always been, and the big best sellers were selling bigger than ever.

Was the market glutted again? Was the distribution system obsolete—especially the ID system, which was having a recession-inflation cash flow problem of its own? Was too much money outstanding in unearned advances to authors?

Trade paperbacks were healthier. In that area, publishers' 1974 receipts of $97.3 million represented a 12.2 percent increase over 1973 and a 39.8 percent increase over 1972. Were trade paperbacks the wave of the future, or was it just that they had not yet reached their own Little Big Horn? Mass market publishers clearly thought that trade paperbacks were at least one wave of the future, and they put more emphasis on a trade kind of publishing.

Introspective, fiercely competitive, sometimes morbidly secretive, mass market paperback publishers were asking themselves these questions in the early months of 1975. There is probably more per capita neurosis in mass market paperbacking than in any other area of book publishing, and the self-doubt is fueled by the large amounts of money that frequently are involved. It seems that practically every week, some paperback industry "statesman" announces that he has a new nostrum that will cure the industry's ills. Everyone knows that the nostrums rarely last very long, but the announcements make everyone uneasy because they think something might be happening that they do not quite understand.

In the late 1940s and early 1950s, the phonograph record industry was in dire trouble. The LP was a new product; firms were recording anything plausible in sight; new companies rose and fell practically overnight; retailers were glutted; unsold records were dumped at disaster prices; composers and musicians were paid irregularly if at all.

Things were never quite that bad with paperbacks, even in the inventory crisis of the 1950s. But the comparison with the record field is not entirely inappropriate. Paperback publishers clearly are in show business: witness all those movie and TV tie-in books. To the show business tradition of "the show must go on " might be added a book publishing tradition: the only thing harder than starting a publishing house is to destroy one that is ongoing. Paperback publishing in America has survived a lot of its obituary writers, and a lot of its practitioners, too.

Whether because of or in spite of the distribution system, paperbacks are everywhere, or so it seems. Their acceptance in mass markets is unquestioned, though the process of getting a specific book to a specific reader can sometimes be messy. As mass markets continue to subdivide into interesting sub-markets that offer profitable opportunities for enterprising publishers, the parameters of everywhere will grow.

It has all come a long way since 1939, when the first Pocket Books were available in only a few major stores in only a few major cities. At that time, if a reader wanted one of those intriguing new PBs but was not near a major store or in a major city, he had to go through a laborious process of ordering the book by mail (cash with order, please). As often as not, he found the process of mailing in some coins (25 cents plus a handling charge) too bothersome, and he went without the book he wanted. Now the book is likely to be available, or can be special ordered, at his nearest drug store or supermarket or shopping center.

It has sometimes been said that there are no more hicks in America. To the extent that that statement may be true, paperbacks can claim a great deal of the credit.

Chapter 14
The Cloudy Crystal Ball

The guess here is that the 1974-75 growth suspension will prove temporary, but that the growth rate in the last half of the decade will be considerably slower than it was in the late 1960s and early 1970s. The danger is that any growth rate may be used as a cosmetic to cover some very serious problems within the paperback industry.

The mass market for books is not really glutted. But certain ways of thinking about the mass market and trying to distribute books to it are showing signs of age.

There is no longer *a* mass market for books; there are many. Just as an author writes a book with specific audiences in mind, the marketing of the book must not lose sight of those specifics. The best paperback publishers have long known this. They have tailor-made their sales, promotion, publicity and advertising efforts and have increasingly adopted a "trade book" publishing approach. But in the paperback industry at large, there is a depressingly pervasive tendency to treat all books alike as though they were all identical loaves of bread that had to be got to the shelves before they turned stale.

An illustration of this dichotomy in industry thinking took place, off the record, at a wholesalers' convention in San Francisco in October 1974. The speaker was Oscar Dystel, president of Bantam Books. He announced that Bantam was ending force-feeding; henceforth wholesalers would receive only those Bantam titles they wanted, and only in those quantities they specifically ordered. He urged other publishers to do the same. Toward the back of the hall, the sales manager of another large paperback house was heard muttering: "I hope they never invite *that* guy to speak again."

The tangible result of force-feeding is waste: returns of unsold books. The intangible result of *not* force-feeding can be underdistribution, but not all books warrant total distribution even if it were possible for all of them. Many books are intended for specific markets within "the" mass market, and they are lost forever if they are just dumped without love into the pipeline that leads to the Big Shredder.

The debate goes on, and the returns pile up. In the first two months of 1975, the AAP reported, mass market publishers' returns increased 18.4 percent. Previously, the industry average for returns had been 36 percent of gross sales—$124.7 million worth of unsold books in 1973—and the range among individual companies was as high as 50 percent. Specifically in the ID sector, wholesalers in 1973 returned 45.4 percent of the books they were shipped. Among publishers, the best performer was little Harlequin Books, with sales of 72.5 percent. Harlequin specializes in inexpensive romances—a sub-mass market—and apparently it does its specialty very well. Among the big firms, Bantam (68.6% sold) performed best, followed by Fawcett (61.2%), Avon (60.6%), Dell (59.8%), Pocket Books (55.8%) and NAL (51.1%). The worst performer sold less than 30 percent of the books it shipped to IDs.

Is anyone doing anything about all this waste? Dystel's program of shipping IDs only what they want is constructive, but it is unlikely, at least at present, that many other firms will follow his banner. Among publishers, his San Francisco speech provoked a rather sour reaction that he was in a position to propose reform because Bantam is so clearly Number One. Bantam got to be Number One, of course, by doing consistently, month after month, a top-quality marketing job with a top-quality mix of books.

Some publishers, surveying the waste in returned books, forecast the end of the ID system. They seem determined to make their prophesies self-fulfilling by taking big accounts—newsstands at a major airport, for example—away from IDs and putting them on a direct basis. This tactic may offer short-term benefits in reducing returns. Its longer-term effect is to undermine the keystone of the distribution structure of mass market publishing. The keystone may no longer be quite so key as it once was, but it is difficult to see how mass publishing could function without it.

Recognizing that, some publishers supplement the IDs' efforts by having their own salesmen check community sales trends, take reorders from retailers and refer the business to the IDs, where the books are locally and quickly available. With less progressive publishers, this is less likely to happen, because their salesmen are credited only for business they send in directly.

Some publishers, surveying the waste in returned books, can afford it because they invest so little in packaging and marketing their books. Such lines are most vulnerable if mass marketing becomes increasingly selective. Meanwhile, ironically it is the ID structure, which is most victimized by the costs of handling the unsuccessful lines, that most sustains them. For an ID, as a *de facto* local franchise, has to take the bottom of a national distributor's line if he wants to continue to profit from the top of the line. He is unlikely to drop a national distributor's line altogether because of its poor quality and performance. If he did, he would soon be facing a competitor in his once-exclusive (or almost exclusive) territory.

93

Each publisher can use his own computerized information on past performances to set realistic print orders, target marketing and thus reduce waste. But as often as not, this information is either ignored or viewed through rose-colored glasses. Among publishers, national distributors and IDs, there has been no cooperative market research, for the industry remains nervous about antitrust laws. The machinery exists for such cooperation. As the mass market continues to fragment, it may become necessary to find ways to use this machinery and still stay within the spirit and letter of the law. The alternative is more waste. It is hard to see how either free enterprise or a free press is well served if, because of antitrust laws, more publishers suffocate in the debris from the shredder.

IDs are less constrained about cooperative ventures to try to open new markets and thus cut waste. Family Reading Centers in supermarkets were the result of IDs' cooperative efforts. In May 1975, a group of IDs formed an association to promote the use of paperbacks in education and invited interested publishers to join them. Some IDs have become educational resource centers in their communities and could become resource centers in other fields as well, such as religion or business management. Some individual IDs are using electronic data processing to learn what they have done in the past, what they are doing at present, and what they should do in the future to target marketing and reduce waste.

That is the good news. The bad news is the many IDs for whom the distribution of books is little more than a knee-jerk.

The ID field at large has some problems. It is an open question whether any of them proves fatal. Selling to widespread chains has produced territorial cross-overs. An ID who once thought he had his territory to himself may suddenly find two or three other IDs working his turf, offering fatter discounts for business from local outlets that the truck driver can serve on his way to and from the local branch of a chain.

There will be more multi-agency ownerships and perhaps another conglomerate or two if more individual IDs find that they must sell out for estate tax or other reasons. Intimations of monopoly exist here. For a multi-agency could use its considerable buying power to demand better discounts, short-cutting the national distribution and threatening a reluctant publisher with a freeze-out of his publications in key cities. This is more likely to happen with magazines than with books. But books could get caught in the fall-out if the multi-ID decided to put a freeze on a national distributor's entire line. The distributor would perhaps retaliate by setting up a competing wholesaler. Shades of the 1920s, the drivers might be riding once again with shotguns under the seat.

The ID field is already embroiled in defending itself against monopoly charges of a somewhat different nature. In May 1974, a special federal grand jury was convened in Atlanta to make a determination on charges brought by the Justice Department's antitrust division that the ID franchise system constituted illegal restraint of trade. The government had already secured a conviction against the ID in New Orleans; three of its officers were fined $50,000 each—the maximum statutory fine—and one was sentenced to a year in jail (eleven months suspended).

In Atlanta, the grand jury heard testimony from retailers, employees of several agencies, people who had tried to get agency franchises and had been denied, publishers' circulation executives, and others. The inquiry ranged widely around the South, but concentrated on situations in Georgia and northern Florida.

IDs have defended the present franchise system on the ground that present territorial patterns were originally imposed by national distributors and publishers in the interests of efficiency in distributing magazines and, later, books. With changes in the antitrust laws, it is doubtful that such a vertical system could be imposed today, but the changes probably could not be applied retroactively. At this time of writing (August 1975), the grand jury was still empanelled.

Thus, in the ID field, two contradictory changes are in the wind—one toward greater monopoly concentration and the other toward breaking up the system. Considering the patchwork nature of the system around the country, conceivably both changes could take place. Change can bring chaos, and either or both of these changes could bring considerable chaos to the distribution of paperback books.

It was perhaps significant that retailers testified in Atlanta. Full-line booksellers and college store managers have a stake in the outcome of the federal court proceedings. Unlike drug stores, newsstands, chain food and variety stores, the bookseller for years has been odd-man-out in mass paperback distribution. The reason is basic: The bookseller wants to order paperbacks title-by-title and set quantities for each title. The ID system is based on force-feeding.

Smaller bookstores and bookstores in geographically removed areas were unable to order books directly from publishers—because economically, the publishers did not want their relatively small orders or because the publishers wanted to support the ID structure. If such booksellers tried to order directly, their orders were referred to the local ID. College booksellers thought themselves particularly victimized because often they were ordering in course-adoption quantities; they could not get from IDs the quantity discounts that a direct-to-publisher order would earn. (It can be argued here that a college store is not entitled to a quanitity discount on such an order because it did not generate the order but is only processing it for a professor.) The situation remained: The publisher could sell, or not sell, to whomever he chose, but the bookseller could not buy from whomever he chose.

More often than not, the bookseller was referred to a local ID whose breadth of stock and bookman's knowledge were insufficient for the bookseller's needs. The ID's discounts were also insufficient to cover a bookstore's operating margins.

A rather extreme case from the mid-1950s illustrates the situation. The bookseller at a major university needed 50 copies each of several titles in a paperback Shakespeare series. When he ordered from the publisher, he was told he would have to order the books through his local ID. Unhappy, he did so. In due course, the books arrived at the ID and were distributed like any other paperbacks. Shakespeare appeared at the city's newsstands, drug stores, bowling alleys—but not at the university. Only after the bookseller documented what had happened was he placed on a direct basis with the publisher. And he had to repeat the process with every other major paperback publisher before he could get on a direct basis with all of them.

Perhaps mindful of the kinds of charges that could come out of an investigation such as the one in Atlanta and perhaps now more eager to short-circuit IDs, publishers are now more willing to give at least a hearing to booksellers who want to buy direct for better discounts. (This discount advantage may prove illusory when one considers the economics of buying, and paying freight charges, from several distant sources vs. buying from one source and getting free local delivery.)

But the burden of proof is still on the bookseller.

First, he has to prove that his local ID is inadequate. Then he has to prove his own financial responsibility, for the publisher will suspect that the bookseller is in arrears with his ID and is looking to direct-from-publisher as a way out of that dilemma. He also has to prove that he is serious about mass market paperbacks by the number of pockets, the feet of rack space or the square footage that he will give to paperbacks, and by the size of the initial order he wants to place (most publishers will accept a minimum of 100 books).

This seems a reasonable liberalization of past practices. But that the issue has become more complex may be seen in this statement in a membership bulletin which the American Booksellers Association issued in February 1975:

97

. . . we continue to hear stories of disturbing efforts by some IDs to discourage or prevent . . . booksellers from opening or continuing direct accounts. We have heard of (1) IDs refusing to sell paperbacks or magazines to booksellers who buy direct from publishers; (2) IDs refusing to sell paperbacks to booksellers who do not buy magazines from them; (3) booksellers being refused direct service from publishers on the ground that all accounts in a given area are serviced by a specified ID; and (4) IDs giving their own retail outlets preferential delivery treatment on items in short supply or enjoying good sales.

If these stories are true, ABA would like documentation. We have been advised by counsel that any of these situations violates the antitrust laws. While the laws and their interpretation are in constant flux, these are some guidelines that any business or association must be wary of violating: using one product as bait for selling another; requiring a customer to buy a product only from you; entering into agreements or gentlemen's understandings dividing up the market or the rejection or termination of customers; giving favored treatment to your own subsidiaries.

According to ABA, this statement produced a sizable volume of sad case histories from its members, giving the association some ammunition for complaint sessions with individual publishers. Out of such sessions may come some constructive solutions to the long vexing situation of how book retailers and mass market publishers will relate to each other. As mass market paperbacks fragment into specialized areas, a good general bookstore is one place where such specialization can be displayed to excellent advantage.

As specialization grows, mass market paperback title production should increase rather than decrease. The next period of paperback history should be one of concentration, not retrenchment. An average per title first printing figure would be meaningless, like adding apples and oranges to get fruit salad. But it is reasonable to expect that a larger percentage of paperbacks than is now the case will be getting smaller printings aimed at smaller, more circumscribed markets.

Rising costs of paper, authors' advances and general overhead have already driven up cover prices. The 75-cent book has all but disappeared. The 95-cent book is an endangered species. An accepted "top" price is now $1.95 for a mass market paperback. Cover prices of $2.25 and $2.50 are becoming increasingly more accepted, especially for books that offer many pages and much entertainment or reference value. The $2.95 price will be seen more and more frequently on such books.

As cover prices go up, literary agents will demand that advances for their authors go up as well. Advances are almost inevitable in this kind of publishing. Because of the nature of distribution, it will be six months or a year from publication before the publisher knows with much certainty how many copies he has actually sold. No author is likely to sit around and wait for the news, especially if he suspects that the news might be bad.

All these factors mean that the initiation fee to mass market paperback publishing is very high. Few new firms are likely to come along and challenge the "Big Five." It would simply take too much money and time to create a challenger. A venture capitalist would be better advised to buy an existing firm, and no doubt the field will see some more of that kind of transaction. The extent to which the "Big Five" dominate the mass paperback field may be seen in figures which CPDA compiled for 1973. Bantam led with 18.1 percent of the market, followed by Dell (11.8%), Fawcett (11.7%), Pocket Books (9.9%), and NAL (9.2%). Avon (5.95%) was sixth, and Warner (4.28%) seventh. Note that these market shares are for *only the ID market,* which, however, is more than half of the total. In specialized markets which increasingly characterize the paperback field, such as juvenile books or religious books or science-fiction or academic books, the market share ranking by company could well be different. But market share statistics *for the ID field* are the only ones publicly available.

Unlike previous paperback rise-and-fall periods, the current period of paperback growth has coincided with the rise of big communications. Both corporately and by the nature of the product and how it is distributed, mass market paperback publishing is part of big communications.

This alliance has provided fiscal and business stability that earlier paperback periods lacked. It also poses threats to editorial creativity and innovation. Best seller thinking now tends to subjugate lesser books to a kind of limbo. Specialist "trade" publishing and marketing provide an antidote. But as the business becomes increasingly expensive, it may be less and less possible for a publisher to afford a few honest mistakes.

If that should happen, a lot of the fun will have gone out of paperback publishing. Among the glories of paperback publishing are those authors who were first published in paperback originals, which were barely reviewed anywhere, and became "household words" in a lot of households after their third or sixth or tenth paperback originals. To name a few such authors: Kurt Vonnegut, Jr., Richard Jessup, R.V. Cassill, Jim Thompson, Donald Hamilton, William Price Fox, John D. MacDonald.

For some, with recognition of their paperbacks has come "graduation" to a more traditional publishing pattern of hardcover first, with attendant reviews, and paperback reprint to follow. MacDonald has gone even further and has seen some of his paperback originals reissued in hardcover, to the accompaniment of retrospective articles in scholarly journals.

These authors won their literary plaudits in hardcover. In paperback, they had already won their audience.

Appendix

"The publishing industry data presented in this appendix were-compiled by *Publishers Weekly* or extracted by *PW* from "AAP Industry Statistics.""

THE MILLION-PLUS PAPERBACKS

As before, we present a list of those titles of which a million or more copies were printed during 1974. Also as before, we have to point out that this does *not* give an accurate indication of numbers of copies actually sold—such figures remain, for the most part, closely guarded secrets. The number of million-plus titles, which rose sharply in 1973, stayed exactly level from 1973 to 1974.

ACE
Love Merchants. 1,000,000

AVON
Sunshine. 1,140,500 (original)
The Wolf and the Dove. 1,250,000 (original)
Secret Life of Plants. 1,050,000

BALLANTINE
How To Be Your Own Best Friend. 2,525,000

BANTAM
The Exorcist. (backlist; total, 11,800,000) 7,100,000
Once Is Not Enough. 3,200,000
Guinness Book of World Records, 12th ed. 3,200,000
Odessa File. 2,325,000
Serpico. 2,275,000
Chariots of the Gods. (backlist; total, 6,200,000) 2,200,000
The Great Gatsby. 2,000,000
White House Transcripts. 1,900,000
Burr. 1,050,000
The Sting. 1,000,000 (original)

BERKLEY
The First Deadly Sin. 1,270,000
Plain Speaking. 1,200,000

FAWCETT
Harvest Home. 1,700,000
The Hollow Hills. 1,450,000
The Curse of the Kings. 1,425,000
Laughing All the Way. 1,200,000
Green Darkness. 1,150,000

The Turquoise Lament. 1,100,000 (original)
Snowfire. 1,050,000
The Final Hour. 1,050,000
The Way to Dusty Death. 1,000,000

DELL
Beulah Land. 2,050,000
The Onion Field. 1,875,000
Presidential Transcripts. 1,700,000
Taking of Pelham One Two Three. 1,550,000
I Heard the Owl Call My Name. 1,050,000

NAL
Fear of Flying. 1,405,000
North Dallas Forty. 1,151,000

POCKET BOOKS
Merriam-Webster Dictionary, (revised ed.) 1,750,000
Papillon. (backlist; total, 2,600,000) 1,100,000
Cosell. 1,025,000

POPULAR LIBRARY
Webster's New World Dictionary. (backlist; total, 17,000,000) 1,000,000

SIMON AND SCHUSTER
The Joy of Sex. 2,628,000

WARNER PAPERBACK LIBRARY
Sybil. 3,300,000
The Camerons. 1,600,000
The Tower. 1,400,000
Upstairs at the White House. 1,200,000
Xaviera Goes Wild. 1,350,250

Source: *Publishers Weekly,* (Feb. 3, 1975), p. 37.

Table 2: Mysteries, Westerns, Science Fiction, Cookbooks
(Both paperback* and hardbound)

Category	1973 New Bks.	New Eds.	Tot.	1974 New Bks.	New Eds.	Tot.
Mysteries	287	85	372	258	148	406
Westerns	60	41	101	93	94	187
Science Fiction	87	26	113	137	77	214
Cookbooks	365	76	441	412	115	527

Table 3: Paperback Titles*
At All Price Levels

Category	1973 New Bks.	New Eds.	Tot.	1974 New Bks.	New Eds.	Tot.
Fiction	741	735	1476	873	945	1818
Non-Fic	5648	2159	7807	7160	2524	9684
Totals:	**6389**	**2894**	**9283**	**8033**	**3469**	**11502**

Included in the above totals are the following:

	1973 New Bks.	New Eds.	Tot.	1974 New Bks.	New Eds.	Tot.
General Fiction	557	594	1151	586	668	1254
Mysteries	117	77	194	145	137	282
Westerns	29	39	68	50	75	125
Science Fiction	38	25	63	92	65	157
Cookbooks	98	44	142	125	64	189
Religious Books	577	167	744	670	196	866

Source: *Publishers Weekly,* (Feb. 3, 1975), p. 39.

Paperback Parnassus

Table 4: Mass Market Paperbacks*

	1973			1974		
Category	New Bks.	New Eds.	Tot.	New Bks.	New Eds.	Tot.
Fiction	615	666	1281	806	889	1695
Non-Fic	373	428	801	457	650	1107
Totals:	**988**	**1094**	**2082**	**1263**	**1539**	**2802**

Included in the above totals are the following:

General Fiction	443	529	972	531	622	1153
Mysteries	107	74	181	142	131	273
Westerns	29	39	68	49	74	123
Science Fiction	36	24	60	84	62	146
Cookbooks	23	17	40	21	25	46
Religious Books	3	15	18	14	27	41

Table 5: Paperbacks Other Than Mass Market*

	1973			1974		
Category	New Bks.	New Eds.	Tot.	New Bks.	New Eds.	Tot.
Fiction	126	69	195	67	56	123
Non-Fic.	5275	1731	7006	6703	1874	8577
Totals	**5401**	**1800**	**7201**	**6770**	**1930**	**8700**

Included in the above totals are the following:

General Fiction	114	65	179	55	46	101
Mysteries	10	3	13	3	6	9
Westerns	0	0	0	1	1	2
Science Fiction	2	1	3	8	3	11
Cookbooks	75	27	102	104	39	143
Religious Books	574	152	726	656	169	825

*Tables 2-5: Judging from mass market industry sources, PW estimates that the **mass market paperback figures printed in these tables should be increased** by as much as 1500 titles over the total which it is possible to report here. For example, the figure 2802 in Table 4 might well be increased to 4300 or thereabouts. PW believes a good part of the increase would come in categories of new light fiction. (See footnote to Table 1.)

Source: *Publishers Weekly,* (Feb. 3, 1975), pp. 39-40.

B—Average Prices, Per Volume, of Mass Market Paperbacks, 1973 and 1974

Category	Total 1973 vols.	Total 1973 prices	Total 1973 Averages	Total 1974 vols.	Total 1974 prices	Total 1974 Averages
Agriculture	10	12.55	1.26	15	21.35	1.42
Art	44	56.20	1.28	61	68.95	1.13
Biography	77	105.80	1.37	118	181.90	1.54
Business	5	7.50	1.50	13	20.70	1.59
Education	11	16.55	1.50	7	11.95	1.71
Fiction	1,305	1,359.70	1.04	1,709	1,991.55	1.17
General Works	15	18.80	1.25	34	46.50	1.37
History	38	54.25	1.43	46	74.80	1.63
Home Economics	60	83.30	1.39	59	91.35	1.55
Juveniles	63	65.55	1.04	113	110.85	.98
Language	9	11.65	1.29	10	13.40	1.34
Law	6	22.15	3.69	8	11.25	1.41
Literature	70	94.70	1.35	96	140.70	1.47
Medicine	53	75.90	1.43	58	89.25	1.54
Music	3	3.95	1.32	1	1.75	1.75
Philosophy, Psychology	89	114.05	1.28	109	144.00	1.32
Poetry, Drama	12	15.90	1.33	20	28.55	1.43
Religion	16	21.45	1.34	38	56.10	1.48
Science	15	23.45	1.56	24	40.65	1.69
Sociology, Economics	118	177.90	1.51	183	293.57	1.60
Sports, Recreation	72	87.50	1.22	127	167.50	1.32
Technology	15	26.35	1.76	14	24.30	1.74
Travel	28	41.50	1.48	38	77.00	2.03
Totals:	**2,134**	**$2,496.65**	**$1.17**	**2,901**	**$3,707.92**	**$1.28**

Source: *Publishers Weekly,* (Feb.3, 1975), p. 4l.

C—Average Prices, Per Volume, of Trade Paper-backs, 1973 and 1974

Category	Total 1973 vols.	Total 1973 prices	1973 Averages	Total 1974 vols.	Total 1974 prices	1974 Averages
Agriculture	66	206.15	3.12	84	343.33	4.09
Art	250	1,082.07	4.33	330	1,512.64	4.58
Biography	177	517.04	2.92	214	685.52	3.20
Business	117	583.05	4.98	201	1,229.66	6.12
Education	417	1,605.07	3.85	420	1,815.18	4.32
Fiction	204	412.84	2.02	127	378.64	2.98
General Works	149	709.92	4.76	232	1,393.40	6.01
History	240	855.80	3.57	246	914.33	3.72
Home Economics	157	423.59	2.70	260	877.71	3.38
Juveniles	202	566.50	2.80	288	530.50	1.84
Language	121	565.51	4.67	183	859.44	4.70
Law	101	504.13	4.99	152	824.53	5.42
Literature	404	1,359.03	3.36	482	1,913.81	3.97
Medicine	339	1,618.77	4.78	452	2,642.71	5.85
Music	54	184.85	3.42	86	409.35	4.76
Philosophy, Psychology	271	876.95	3.24	388	1,543.95	3.98
Poetry, Drama	382	1,025.38	2.68	439	1,309.85	2.98
Religion	572	1,544.16	2.30	770	2,087.64	2.71
Science	394	2,343.92	5.95	612	4,557.87	7.45
Sociology, Economics	1,439	5,420.18	3.77	1,676	7,672.26	4.58
Sports, Recreation	287	799.82	2.79	307	981.73	3.20
Technology	263	1,913.44	7.28	364	2,040.50	5.61
Travel	362	1,231.77	3.40	418	1,679.02	4.02
TOTALS:	**7,068**	**$26,349.94**	**$3.73**	**8,731**	**$38.203.57**	**$4.38**

Source: *Publishers Weekly* (Feb. 3, 1975), p. 4l.

Table I

Estimated Book Publishing Industry Sales by AAP Survey Categories*

MILLIONS OF DOLLARS

	1971	1972	1973	1974	Percent Change From '73	Percent Change From '72
	$	$	$	$		
Trade (Total)	422.7	442.0	460.1	522.7	13.6	23.6
Adult Hardbound	242.0	251.5	264.8	308.2	16.4	27.3
Adult Paperbound	69.6	79.6	86.7	97.3	12.2	39.8
Juvenile	111.1	110.9	108.6	117.2	7.9	5.5
Religious (Total)	108.5	117.5	124.7	130.6	4.7	20.4
Bibles, Testaments, Hymnals & Prayer-books	54.4	61.6	66.5	67.5	1.5	24.1
Other Religious	54.1	55.9	58.2	63.1	8.4	16.6
Professional (Total)	353.0	381.0	405.4	466.3	15.0	32.1
Technical & Scientific	122.3	131.8	138.4	158.3	14.4	29.4
Business & Other Professional	178.3	192.2	206.2	236.3	14.6	32.5
Medical	52.4	57.0	60.8	71.7	17.9	36.8
Book Clubs	229.5	240.5	262.4	283.6	8.1	23.6
Mail Order Publications	194.6	198.9	221.2	247.0	11.7	26.9
Mass Market Paperback	228.8	252.8	285.9	293.6	2.7	28.3
University Presses	39.3	41.4	42.6	46.1	8.2	17.3
Elementary & Secondary Text	496.6	497.6	547.9	598.8	9.3	20.1
College Text	371.5	375.3	392.2	453.4	15.6	19.6
Standardized Tests	25.3	26.5	28.8	34.2	18.7	25.2
Subscription Reference	301.0	278.9	262.2	280.2	6.8	−6.9
Other	141.0	154.8	164.2	176.0	7.2	24.8
Total	**2911.8**	**3007.2**	**3197.6**	**3532.5**	**10.5**	**20.9**

*Extracted from "AAP 1974 Industry Statistics," Table S3.

Source: *Publishers Weekly* (Jul. 14, 1975), p. 26.

Table III

Estimated 1974 Sales of Books and Materials in the Educational Market: Domestic Sales

MILLIONS OF DOLLARS

	Total Market		ELHI Textbooks		College Textbooks		AV and Other Media		Mass Market Paperbacks		General Books		Subscription Reference Books		Maps		Standardized Tests	
	$	%†	$	%	$	%	$	%	$	%	$	%	$	%	$	%	$	%
ELHI	1015	100	503	50	20	2	228	22	43	4	169	17	13	1	11	1	28	3
College	758	100	39	5	361	48	19	3	28	4	304	40	4	*	2	*	1	*
Total	$1773	100	$542	31	$381	21	$247	14	$71	4	$473	27	$17	*	$13	*	$29	2

†Percent Share of Market.
*Denotes less than 1 percent

Extracted from AAP report, Table T2. Data for "AV and Other Media" are supplied to AAP by Educational Media Producers Council, National Audiovisual Association.

Source: *Publishers Weekly* (Jul. 14, 1975), p. 27.

Index

Ace Books, 73
advertising, radio &
TV, 57
advertising, space, 57
Albatross Books, 67, 71
American Booksellers
Association, 2 97-8
American News Com-
pany, 15-17
Anchor Books, 77-8
antitrust laws, 44, 93
ARA Services, Inc., 20-1
art directors, 30
Association of American
Publishers (AAP), 10,
22, 26, 40, 41, 92
Atheneum, 79
Australia, 45-6
automatic stripping
machine, 25
Avon Books, 71, 75-6, 92,
99

backlist business, 37
Ballantine, Ian, 71, 74-5
Ballantine Books, 74-5
Bantam Books, 16, 72,
75-6, 92-3, 99
Berkley Books, 73, 75
best sellers, 35
bids, 50, 52-3
Big Shredder, 23, 26
Blockbuster Books, 51
Book-of-the-Month
Club, 72

books that no longer
have covers, 27
bookstore chains, 18
branch warehouses, 36
British Publishers Association, 44

Canada, 45, 46-7
CBS, 75
chains, 35
chains, variety, 17, 30
Charles Levy agency,
29-30
Cheap Libraries, 66
Cirker, Hayward, 78
Computer Book Service,
30
Crowell, Cedric, 69
Council for Independent
Distribution (CID), 17
Council for Periodical
Distributors Associa-
tions (CPDA), 18, 26,
28, 30, 36-7, 99
cover art, 56
cover artists, 56
covers, 43, 74
covers that never had
books, 27
Curtis Circulation
Company, 71

de Graff, Robert Fair,
68-9
Dell, 16-7, 71, 76, 92, 99

department stores, 30
dime novels, 66
District News Company, 20, 64
The Dopey Club, 51-4
Doubleday, 77
Dover Publications, 77-8
Durant, Will, 67

Enoch, Kurt, 71, 73
Epstein, Jason, 78

Family Reading Centers, 18, 94
Fawcett, 73, 76, 92, 99
Federal Trade Commission (FTC), 20-1
Field, Marshall, 70
food stores, 30
force-feeding, 22, 29, 57
Frankfurt Book Fair, 47

Grosset & Dunlap, 71-2
Gulf & Western Industries, 75

Haldemann-Julius, E., 66
W.F. Hall Printing Company, 62
Harcourt Brace Jovanovich, 75
Harlequin Books, 92
Harper & Brothers, 72
Hearst, 75
Howe, Wallis E. Jr., 16-7

independent wholesaler (ID) 11-3, 15, 18-22, 25-6, 33-5, 37, 80, 93-8
Infantry Journal, 71
international copyright agreement, 66
"instant books," 61
Intext, 75
Istituto Finanziario Industriale (IFI), 76

jobber, 11, 13, 19

Jovanovich, William, 75
Justice, U.S. Dept. of, 44

Kramer, Sidney, 71

Lane, Allen, 67
Library of Congress, 84
literary agent, 51
Little Blue Books, 66
Little, Brown & Co., 72
E.T. Lowe Publishing Company, 62
Los Angeles Times-Mirror, 75

Market Rights Agreement, 44
Mentor, 73
Modern Age Books, 67
Modern Library, 78
Morton, Joe, 17
movie and TV tie-ins, 42, 50, 53
National Association of College Stores (NACS), 2, 80
national distributor, 11-2
National General Corporation, 76
New American Library (NAL), 16, 73, 75-6, 92 99
New York State Supreme Court, 28
New York Times Book Review, 84
news butchers, 15
newspaper circulation wars, 16

Oceana Publications, 78
originals, 47

"package" of titles, 54
paperback jobber, 18
paperback rights, 50-50
split of, 53
paperback rights auctions, 51, 54

Paperback Library, 75
Paperbound Books in
    Print (PBIP), 5, 84
Peacock Press, 75
Penguin Books, 67
Pitkin, Walter, Jr., 71
Pocket Books, 16-7, 53,
    65-70, 74-6, 92-99
points of sale, 19
Popular Library, 16-7,
    71, 75
Frederick A. Praeger,
    Inc., 79
"promotion allowances,"
    31
Publishers Weekly, 84-5
G. P. Putnam, 75
Pyramid Books, 73, 75

race track wire services,
    15
radio and TV advertising,
    57
Random House, 72, 75
Regensteiner Press, 62-3
retailers, 20
retitling of older books,
    31
returns, 22, 26
Robbins, Harold, 53
Rocky Mountain News
    Company, 17

Saypol, Judge Irving H.,
    28
Scholastic Magazines,
    Inc., 10
school business, 35, 37
Schuster, M. Lincoln, 68
Scribners, 72
Shimkin, Leon, 70
Signet, 73
Simon & Schuster, 28,
    67-8
smutty covers, 31
space advertising, 57
Strachan & Henshaw, 63

subsidiary rights, 50
"suggested allotments,"
    22

"talk" shows, radio and
    TV, 50
Tauchnitz Editions, 67
territorial rights, 15
"tip" sheets, 15
Traditional Market
    Rights Agreement, 44,
    45
Trident Press, 53
truck driver (ID's), 29, 34

Universal Copyright Con-
    vention, 44
Universal Product Code
    (UPC), 30

variety chains, 17, 30

Warner Communica-
    tions, 75
Warner Paperback, 75-6,
    99
Watergate tapes, 62
Weybright, Victor, 71
    73